America's Discrimination Circus

Author: Kathleen Brush

Dedication
To all Americans that know America is the greatest
nation on earth for people of all colors and creeds.

A special thanks to Jack Colbeck, P.T. Caso, Bruce Coleman, John Bianchi
and Boots Caso for their unvarnished input on how improve this booklet.

Table of Contents

Introduction

"Everybody has asked the question…What shall we do with the Negro?' I have had but one answer from the beginning. Do nothing with us! Your doing with us has already played the mischief with us…And if the negro cannot stand on his own legs. Let him fall. All I ask is, give him a chance to stand on his own legs." What the Black Man Wants. Frederick Douglas, 1865.[1]

Blacks were left too alone. Or were they? Jim Crow laws segregated blacks in the south, where more than 90% of blacks lived. It took a little time, but blacks clearly demonstrated that it was freedom, not whites, that they needed to stand on their own legs. In the 1940s, the poverty rate for blacks was 87%. In 1960, the poverty rate was 47%.[2,3]

In 1964, something extraordinary occurred. For centuries, white supremacy was evident in parts of the world, just like Chinese supremacy, Yoruba supremacy, Sunni Muslim supremacy, and Russian supremacy was apparent in other parts. Most kept their supremacy, but America did not. White men dominated the American leadership landscape until the middle of the 20th century, but then something occurred that was unprecedented in world history. They decided it wasn't fair, and they voluntarily relinquished power. Between 1964 and 1970, white Americans unequivocally denounced a racist past and committed to an anti-racist future. Anyone that truly aspired to be successful, would not be denied due to their race, color, sex, religion, or national origin.

President Johnson went one giant step further. He decided to help blacks stand on their own legs. In 1965, he presided over the launch of the War on Poverty programs with the aim "not only to relieve the symptoms of poverty, but to cure it and, above all, to prevent it." Enumerated keys to success included giving people better education and training, in addition to health care and "decent communities." A benevolent mission. A delusional mission for an institution – government - that is commonly described as dysfunctional, ineffective, corrupt, unprincipled, and biased.

In 1964, people of all races, colors, and national origin were given legal protections to enable a level competitive playing field. A playing field that has been responsible for millions to bask in the admiration of being rags-to-riches self-made people. In 1965, that formula was changed. Instead of people being forced to improve their educations and skills and working hard to better provide for themselves and their families, people now had an option *not* to stand on their own legs.

Since 1965, the cost of War on Poverty programs has increased on average 7.4% annually.[4] Today, they have an annual price tag of about $1.1 trillion. In 2018, black poverty was 20.8%, a decrease of 1.3% from 2000. For Latinos it was 17.6%, a decrease of 3.6% from 2000.[5,6] In eighteen years, about 901,000 people have been raised from poverty, or about 1.2% of a 68 million annual population of welfare recipients. Based on a $1.1 trillion annual spend, the cost to American taxpayers to lift one person from poverty is about *$22 million.* [7,8,9] Not only have War on Poverty programs failed to cure poverty they have resulted in many unintended consequences, such as worsened public safety, reduced economic growth, and millions self-selecting slavery 2.0. The latter is a reference to people being dependent on government handouts. A significant contributor to the failures of the War on Poverty programs is the incapacity of American governments, even with trillions of dollars, to raise the education and skill levels of recipients to a level that motivates them to want to stand on their own legs.

Poverty pimps and race hustlers. According to the late African American Professor Walter Williams, diminished progress for blacks is an outcome of opportunistic poverty pimps and race hustlers conjuring up white guilt with a narrative of blacks as victims of white oppression. [i] War on Poverty programs offered billions and even trillions of reasons to pimp and hustle. In spite of an America that bore no resemblance to its racist past these opportunists found it easy to conjure up white guilt by pretending that Jim Crow was alive and well. One opportunity led to the next. In 1987, Tawana Brawley, a young black girl was found with racial slurs written on her body. She was covered in feces, allegedly sexually assaulted, and found in a garbage bag. Her alleged attackers included a white cop and a white prosecutor. Her story quickly started unravelling as a hoax. That was not a deterrent to the circus acts surrounding it. The ringmaster was Al Sharpton. He had blacks cheering wildly as he hurled false accusations about whites, and whites cowered. Sharpton is as good as it gets for dividing blacks and whites and parlaying a post-60's identity of keeping whites "on the hook." [10,11]

Twenty years later, Chrystal Magnum, a black female college student and stripper accused three white Duke lacrosse players of rape. Jesse Jackson became the lead hustler. He characterized America in the 21st century as no different than the 17th and 18th centuries of plantations and slavery. "The history of white men and black women – the special fantasies and realities of exploitation – goes back to the nation's beginning and the arrival of slaves from Africa." The lead prosecutor on this case, a white man, knew almost immediately that the lacrosse players were innocent, but he kept the case alive. He said: "The circumstances of the rape indicated a deep racial motivation for some of the things that were done." He was accused of pandering to black constituents, and he was re-elected. [12]

Media broadcasts of the horrific allegations of Jussie Smollett went 24x7. It appeared that Jim Crow was alive and well in 2019. Two white men yelling racial and homophobic slurs placed a noose around his neck and poured bleach on him. Wearing MAGA hats, no one doubted the story. Smollett received an outpouring of support from all over the country. Jesse Jackson called it a "barbaric lynching" and bellowed "hate and violence are raining down on our country." Black Senator Cory Booker called it a "modern day lynching." Black actress Grace Byers said: "This despicable act only shamefully reveals how deeply the diseases of hatred, inequality, racism, and discrimination continue to course through our country's veins." Black comedian Steve Harvey said: "Another brother that has tasted the brutality of hatred, racism and bigotry." African American Congressman Bobby Rush called the police uncovering the hoax, "the sworn enemy of black people." The nation was gripped by this horrific saga. The shaming of conservatives as white supremacists was relentless.

Falsely shaming America and Americans was irrelevant to the quick decision by Cook County State's Attorney Kim Foxx to drop the charges against hoaxer Smollett. The Chicago Mayor blasted Foxx for not adhering to rule of law by applying double standards. [13] Foxx wondered if the rancor was because she was African American. Before new

---

[i] Williams said: "Racial discrimination and racism in our country could have earned a well-deserved death, but it has been resurrected by race hustlers or poverty pimps as I call them, such as Jesse Jackson, Al Sharpton and many others in the civil rights movement who make a living on the grievance of Blacks."

charges were pressed for fabricating a hate crime and lying to police hubristic Smollett contemplated suing the police because of racism. But why were Smollett and his supportive hustlers spared the career-killing label of racist? [14, 15]

The hangman's knot on the garage door pull in race car driver Bubba Wallace's garage gave way to instant cries of NASCAR as a sport for white supremacists. Hustler Sharpton seized the moment. "To hang a noose, which is a symbol of lynching and killing somebody because of the color of their skin, shows real hatred and real bigotry….that's why we're marching all over the country." [16] NASCAR fans, drivers, and whites all over the country gave an outpouring of condemnation for the incident and unqualified support for Wallace – not hatred or bigotry. Fans tweeted #IStandWithBubba. Turns out the hangman's knot on the garage-door pull had been there for months.

In 2020, New Orleans Saints quarterback white Drew Brees tried to defend America by saying he believed "we should all stand for the national anthem and respect our country." He was skewered by professional athletes and hustlers. African American teammate Malcolm Jenkins said: "Our communities are under siege, and we need help… sometimes you should shut the f--- up." African American Hall of Famer Ed Reed said: "I see Drew Brees trying to do his part to bring black folk down..." Brees, the alleged oppressor, apologized: "It breaks my heart to know the pain I have caused."[17]

Brees felt compelled to apologize for standing up for America. The multi-millionaire black athletes, actors, politicians, pimps, hustlers, and "social justice advocates" that have falsely accused white people as racists, called America racist, and pretend that America in 1800 is America in the late 20th and early 21st century have refused to apologize. Race trumps all. Besides, hustlers can't apologize because that lets whites off the hook.

The ability to post cell phone video clips of blacks and whites engaged in something allegedly racist have created armies of opportunistic poverty pimps and race hustlers. The media carries their water and now there are daily reminders of what has become the uncontestable but false narrative of white oppression and black victimhood. Every new video clip of a policeman engaged with a black person sends social media into a frenzy, often followed by protests or riots. Cities have been devastated. It's not just police; one-sided videos are regularly posted anytime a white person says or does something a black or woke person interprets as racist. A young girl that tells a group of young black men that are repetitive diners-and-dashers that they have to pay for their food before they get it, was made into a vile racist by African American Masud Ali, a self-proclaimed "victim," of racial stereotyping. The girl's employer, Chipotle, reflexively fired her and apologized to the world for her behavior. Ali's video was watched nearly 7 million times overnight and it was aired on ABC television. Headlines blasted Chipotle for racial profiling. Ali's tweets showed him to be a braggart about stealing food from restaurants. Chipotle was aware of this, but they still assumed their white employee was a racist and a young black man an innocent victim.

Race baiting has become very powerful for pimps and hustlers. Ironically, it first became part of American life when racism in America became characterized as residual. For the pimps and hustlers, racism cannot be residual because they rely on a false narrative of systemic racism for black power. This is why they have been goading whites into thinking that racism in America today is no different than the days of the Jim Crow south when stores hung signs saying no colored folks allowed.

Uncle Tom. In 2008, then presidential candidate Barack Obama appealed to blacks to stand on their own legs. "Children who grow up without a father are five times more likely to live in poverty and commit crime; nine times more likely to drop out of schools and twenty times more likely to end up in prison." We need "families to raise our children. We need fathers to realize that responsibility does not end at conception. We need them to realize that what makes you a man is not the ability to have a child — it's the courage to raise one. We need to help all the mothers out there who are raising these kids by themselves…Their children need another parent. That's what keeps their foundation strong. It's what keeps the foundation of our country strong." The response to Obama from never-let-the-whites-off-the-hook hustler Jesse Jackson was he wanted "to cut his nuts out," and "accused him of talking down to black people."[18]

A black person encouraging blacks to stand on their own legs has become an Uncle Tom. Hustlers want to cut off their nuts. The brilliant black neurosurgeon Ben Carson preached self-reliance and encouraged blacks to get educated and to see success as something they controlled. Carson became a favorite whipping boy for black comedian Trevor Noah. Noah threw insults at the erudite and articulate Carson to solidify the message that he was acting white. A portrait of Carson with the words: "The person who has the most to do with your success is you," was removed from a school entrance in Baltimore. The principal said his message feels hostile. [19] Ben Carson became Dr. Uncle Tom. He had the good company of Martin Luther King. He too has been called Uncle Tom. His civil approach to improving race relations has the distinct appearance of acting white.

Obama's message on two-parent families was a good one and for all Americans. At 23%, America has the highest percentage of single parent households in the world. [20] In 2019, according to the US Census, 18% of Latino households were single parent, whites 11%, Asians 7%, and blacks 64%. For blacks, this was an increase of 42 points since 1965. The rate of poverty for any racial/ethnic group is greatly influenced by the proportion of families that have one or two parents in a household. In 2018, the poverty rate for blacks was 20.8%, Latinos 17.6%, and whites and Asians 10.1%.[ii] The poverty rate for married couples or double income cohabitating couples across races has been 7-7.5%. Poverty has ties to a host of problems, like higher crime rates and lower educational and health outcomes.[21,22,23]

White House hustling. While running for president, Barack Obama distanced himself from his spiritual adviser, Jeremiah Wright, who openly preached God damn America and accused the US of creating HIV to eradicate blacks. He wasn't however distancing himself from community organizing. In office, he outsourced activism to Al Sharpton, America's grandest race baiter. The team of Obama, Sharpton, and Attorney General Eric Holder succeeded in building the narrative of a systemically racist criminal justice system fueled by racist cops. Data didn't support the narrative. What it did support was skyrocketing violent and non-violent crime by blacks in single parent families. The narrative of racist cops persisted anyway. Obama denied he started the war on cops. Most know if he didn't start it, he poured gas on it every chance he got, and it's working. In 2020, 336 officers were killed in the line of duty. That's a 57% increase over the five-year average. Out of office, Obama is still fueling the war on cops. The Obama foundation website states, "Over 1,000 people are killed by police every year in America, and Black people are three times

---

[ii] The census did not offer data on Native American single parent households, but the poverty rate is 25.4%, and 54% of Native American children live in single parent households.

more likely to be killed than White people." (In 2020 blacks were 2.3 times more likely.)[24] Is this an indicator of racist cops? Why is the reality that blacks are 3.7 times more likely to engage with police because of violent crime omitted from the racist cop narrative? The bigger problem is the phony allusion of cops arbitrarily and regularly killing black people.

Many will surely be surprised to know that in 2019 the probability of a black person being killed by a cop when they *are* engaging in a crime but *unarmed and not* seriously threatening police is less than the chance of being struck by lightning. [25,26] Are you wondering how it can be that the narrative of marauding racist killer cops has been digested as a truism? Or have you heard it so many times in the media, including social media, that you too thought it was true?

There is no shortage of people with a pen participating in the war on cops. That shouldn't detract from the reality that people of any color strolling along the street are not killed by police. Police kill criminals when they fear for their lives. An officer is 5 times more likely to be killed on the job than a criminal is to be killed by an officer, 3.2 times more likely to be killed by a black person.[27,28]

The Obama foundation further implores people to learn about police violence. Nothing is said about: blacks being 6 times more likely than whites to murder someone; blacks being 10 times more likely to murder a white person than vice versa; or blacks being 13.4% of the population but responsible for more than half of all murders in the nation. [29,30] This data would indicate that blacks are disproportionately violent, but the foundation's narrative is about police violence that is triggered solely by an inaccurate stereotype that blacks are dangerous.

Nobel Peace Prize winner Obama would do the nation, the black community and the police a real service by running a headline on the Obama Foundation website that said: The probability of a black person minding his own business being killed by a cop is the same for whites, Latinos, Asians, and Native Americans. Zero.

Obama didn't completely outsource hustling to Sharpton. He could hustle too. When conservatives wanted people to show ID in order to vote he indicated conservatives were reviving Jim Crow. Reviving Jim Crow and slavery are potent weapons in the pimp and hustler arsenal. Obama steered clear of noting that conservatives couldn't revive Jim Crow laws because these were the laws of politically left-leaning states. Conservative opposition to the Jim Crow laws was a reason the KKK targeted conservatives.[31, 32] When Obama "the racial healer" and peace-prize winner left office, race relations had worsened by a margin of 3:1. [33] But the pimps and hustlers were as powerful as ever.

Black Lives Matter's hustlers and pimps. Black Live Matter (BLM) was born in the Obama era. Defund the police became a BLM platform issue. A common criticism of BLM is that they focus on some black lives mattering more than others. For example, why is the focus on the lives of the 235 blacks that were killed by police in 2019, of which 97.4% were armed or threatening the lives of police? There were 25 times more blacks killed by blacks in 2019. [34] Another BLM platform issue is degrading the importance of the "white" nuclear family structure. How does that support black lives mattering? Single parent black households have been a significant contributor to blacks having the lowest performance in education and the highest performance in crime, poverty, and social welfare of any racial/ethnic group. On nuclear families, Obama seems to have gone silent. Advisor Sharpton may have influenced Obama to prioritize keeping whites on the hook over encouraging blacks to stand on their own legs.

During the summer of 2020, when the nation experienced 557 riots involving BLM activists,[35] many Americans expressed sympathy for the plight of black "victims." As victims, politicians began absolving rioters and other activists of legal responsibility for crimes they committed. There was an estimated $2 billion in property damage. Americans were told this was equity. This was social justice. Political leaders might have had the added motivation of Black Live's Matter (BLM) leaders and hustlers like Hawk Newsome that threatened, "If this country doesn't give us what we want, then we will burn down this system and replace it."[36] Newsome, like BLM leader, Alicia Garza, was pretty sure they would prevail in getting what they wanted because Democratic leaders were avidly supporting the "mostly peaceful protests." [iii] The protests, etc., could provide leverage for them to pass new laws and spending programs.[37,38] Garza said, "the response of Democratic Party officials to every outbreak of violence—bearing new programs and opening new veins of spending—connected activism and revolt." [39] Democrats don't do this for free. This is a *quid pro quo* relationship. In exchange for "new veins of spending," blacks cement their Democratic voting block and financially support Democratic candidates. Through the ActBlue PAC, BLM funneled billions into democratic candidates in the 2020 elections.[40]

Congressional poverty pimps. One ActBlue recipient is Latina Congresswoman Alexandra Ocasio-Cortez (AOC). She and her fellow Democratic Socialist Party members count among the most effective poverty pimps. Many core beliefs of this party are consistent with Marxism/ socialism/ communism.[iv] The position of the Democratic Socialists is that they don't value equality of opportunity; they want equality of outcomes. The now oft-heard phrases of equity and equitable solutions is doublespeak for socialism with an aim of delivering equality of outcomes. Equity is also a euphemism for legalizing discrimination against hardworking, self-reliant, law-abiding people.

The Democratic Socialists have plenty of supporters. Nearly 20% of millennials support socialism. There is something attractive about free lunches, or is it free college and health care? That's a 500% increase over people that lived through the Cold War and know how socialism destroys private property, the will of people to achieve, and ultimately countries. The last year China embraced a socialist economic system was 1978. According to the IMF, per capita income in China in 1978 was $156. In the United States it was $10,588. Socialism did and does, however, deliver equity and social justice. People are equally poor, and no one has an opportunity to change that. Voila – income inequality is extinguished.

The people of color hustle. A giant ploy of the hustlers and pimps is the creation of the euphemism, people of color (POC). For decades, POC has been presented as a unified bloc of victims. It was said that in the mid-21st century when POC became the new majority they would exact discriminatory revenge on whites. Revenge for implementing laws, policies, and programs to create an unparalleled anti-racist multiracial nation? White

---

[iii] African American Congresswoman Ayanna Pressley said: "There needs to be unrest in the streets for as long as there's unrest in our lives." African American VP Kamala Harris: "Everyone should take note of that, on both levels, that they're not going to let up — and they should not. And we should not." And "if you are able to, chip in now to the #MNFreedomFund to help post bail for those protesting on the ground in Minnesota." In Minnesota, about 1300 properties were damaged, 100 near-destroyed, and the damage estimate was $500 million. Protests and riots became ordinary in Seattle in the 2nd half of 2020. White Seattle Mayor Jenny Durkan blamed the riots on privileged white men. Durkan then allocated $100 million to BIPOC communities from a city coffer that was empty.

[iv] Marxism, socialism and communism are all socialist systems, and the terms are commonly used interchangeably.

Americans should not lose any sleep. There is no unified POC bloc. Many Latinos are white and 88% self-identify as white. When it comes to improving educational outcomes, working hard and taking entrepreneurial risks, Latinos are behaving similarly to Italian immigrants, somewhat tempered by access to welfare. Latinos also have a little problem sitting under the big tent of POC victims. Their "black history" is no different than Americas, except the prevalence of slavery and racism was far more extensive and the latter remains alive and well. America purchased 3-4% of the slaves in the Atlantic slave trade and Latin America 96-97%. If white Americans have been tagged as oppressors due to a tiny percentage of people that have ancestors that were enslavers, non-black Latinos are oppressors too – definitely not victims. Asians don't qualify as victims either and this has nothing to do with slavery. Asians are a race all their own that quickly grasped how to achieve success in America -- adopt the American Creed. This means working hard, obeying the law, speaking English, and becoming educated and self-reliant. Asian success is why some have begun grouping Asians with whites. When Asians protested, they were lumped into the privileged group – white implied. Latino, Asian, and American realities have diluted the power of waving the inevitable revenge of the alleged POC victims.

It turns out that POC is moving on, and BIPOC is its replacement. BIPOC is a catchy acronym where blacks and indigenous populations are separated from POC, and B takes center stage. Black Lives Matter created even more POC separation. BLM cares naught about POC only BI. If it seems odd for BLM to include "I" because Native Americans enslaved blacks,[41] that is blamed on "I" being forced to act white. Being forced to act white is the same excuse blacks give to Africans that were responsible for selling 35-215 million slaves to traders for transport to other continents, including 388,000 to the United States.[42,43]

White guilt? Poverty pimps and race hustlers have done a grave disservice to Americans of all colors. Blacks suffer the most because many have come to believe they are victims of white oppression. White guilt encourages this. According to the US Census, just 1.25% of Americans in 1860 held slaves, but many whites have come to feel guilty about slavery. Only in America could people in the 21st century be made to feel personally guilty for slavery that was abolished in the 19th century, and for systemic racism that was obliterated in the mid-20th century. People feeling guilty about people they didn't know, things they had nothing to do with and never would have supported. Things America has diligently corrected and has done so in a manner unique in the world.

There is no country that has provided more opportunities for minority groups or has strived harder to deliver equality of opportunity. America had systemic racism in the past, but it is no more. The United States has created an enduring anti-racist nation that Americans can take pride in. There is nothing to feel guilty about and nothing to be on the hook for. If some groups want to compete in a Victimhood Olympics, whites can do nothing to end the contest. Trying to help is an invitation to being called a white supremacist. Putting an end to a belief in victimhood is a job for the ethnic and political leaders that are perpetuating it. They created it and only they can solve it.

Book flow. In the pages that follow there is an exploration of what drives America's discrimination circus. Spoil alert. It's not discrimination. We'll look at how the nation with the most successful minority populations in the world, can be cast as a nation of victims. Then we'll move to the untested and untestable Critical Race Theory (CRT) and other 1980s snake oil that has captured the hearts and minds of legions of social justice advocates. The inane concept of white privilege is covered and so is a black aversion to acting white, which includes valuing education. The race hustlers and poverty pimps feature in a chapter on benevolent racism. This is where "well-meaning" people "inadvertently" reinforce racial domination.

Three chapters debunk the claims of racist health care, education, and criminal justice systems by showing, for example, the influence that bad health habits have on disproportional health outcomes, or the influence that anti-intellectualism and political support for the teachers' unions have on disproportional education outcomes, and the influence of criminal behaviors on disproportional run-ins with the police. In the chapter, The Oxymoronic Rule of Law, the morphing of America's legal system from one which endeavors to see all people as equal in the eyes of the law, to one that divides people into victims and privilege is explored. For victims there is social justice, for the others there is legal justice or no justice. Also covered is the utter insanity of centering American history around slavery per Project 1619, living up to a commitment to equality of opportunity and a dangerous complacency toward separate but equal. Throughout the book the different rationales for systemic racism, including the original sin of slavery, the original sin of racism, the fugitive slave clause in the constitution, and the presence of humans with unconsciously biased thoughts are examined.

Pimps, hustlers, well-meaning misinformed social justice advocates, and people harboring guilt for being born white have taken the leading anti-racist nation and falsely portrayed it into a racist pariah. It is the story of America's Discrimination Circus. It is the story of the world's greatest con job.

We are all victims

Discrimination, discrimination, discrimination. It's impossible to go through a news hour without another report of discrimination. In 2006 the focus was on discrimination against illegal immigrants; most were Latinos. In 2013, with the inception of the Black Lives Matter movement, the focus was on discrimination against blacks. In 2015, stories of discrimination focused on LGBTQ. In 2017, #MeToo accentuated discrimination against women in the form of sexual harassment. In 2020, discrimination against blacks rose to the forefront. Drowning in a sea of discriminatory allegations, it would be impossible to know that America has the most successful female and minority populations in the world.

-African Americans are the most prosperous and educated black population in the world. They also have the highest household income of all but one of the fifty black majority-nations.[v] If African Americans had their own nation, they would have the 15th largest GDP in the world. African American GDP is three times larger than Nigeria, the African country with the largest GDP. Nigeria has four times as many people.

-The GDP of US Latinos is higher than any country in Latin America. This includes Brazil, which has three times as many people. Latino household income is also higher than exists in any Latin American (Latam) nation. If American-Latinos had their own GDP it would be the eighth largest in the world, and of the top ten economies, it would be the third fastest growing.

-No indigenous population has been courted more to ensure fair compensation for their land or received the protected freedoms, concessions, and financial transfers as Native Americans.

-Asian Americans are the most educated and most highly compensated racial group in America. They average 25% greater household income than whites. Asians from India are the most successful of all. They average 60% higher household income than whites.

-Of the 100 most influential women in the world, 46 are American. Second place goes to China with nine. Five black women are on the list. Four are from the United States and one is from Barbados. Five of the top ten richest women in the world are American.

This type of data takes many by surprise because the media has painted the United States as a hell hole of discrimination.

In this hell hole, is there anyone that doesn't face discrimination? The belief used to be that white men over 5'9" but less than 6'4" that went to an Ivy League school, were average weight, Protestant, under 40, and wealthy escaped discrimination. That's no longer true. If anyone doubted this, it was put to bed when then President-elect Joe Biden announced his priorities for dispensing Covid-19 aid. Everyone was a priority but white men. [44] In the midst of a nation undergoing ultra-heightened attention to discrimination,

---

[v] The Bahamas has higher household incomes. It has <1% of the Americas black population. Significant revenue comes from being a tax haven and from corporations attracted to financial secrecy.

Biden was casual about a blatantly discriminatory policy against white men. Still, his racist position wasn't as bad as governments in the Pacific Northwest that prioritized Covid aid to BIPOC. [45] That excludes white men and women. Why not just call BIPOC non-white, so people don't have to look up what it stands for?

Many thought Biden's announcement was really targeting white male conservatives, and by accident an equal number of white left-leaning men got caught in the snare. You know what? No one cares about white successful men that are left, right or moderate facing discrimination. It's really kind of crummy because 80% of these guys are self-made and had to work really hard for their success. Now they face discrimination. [46] White men that work hard and innovate are no longer applauded. These are chalked off to privilege, and that's a basis for discrimination. It's not just successful white men that face discrimination for being privileged, all white people do. There are twice as many whites living in poverty as blacks, but all whites are privileged and oppressors, even if they are dirt poor. White men could not have guessed that taking the unprecedented act of opening up the nation in 1964 to make sure anyone that truly aspired to be successful would not be denied this opportunity due to discrimination based on race, color, sex, religion, or national origin, would later result in what seems like legal discrimination against people of the white race.

Discrimination against white people is overt. Exclude whites (including Jews[vi]), and overt racial discrimination has virtually disappeared. Overt discrimination against whites is illegal too, but no one cares about that. Let's call that white un-privilege. The new enemy number one in the alleged war on racism is covert discrimination, of course not against white people. It is covert discrimination against non-whites in the form of unconsciously biased thoughts. The perceptions of these thoughts underlie one of the revised definitions of systemic racism and the one that pervades most allegations and innuendos of racist America.

Let's take a look under the covers of the supposed hell hole of discrimination. No one faces more discrimination than fat people. It's inevitable that a fat person will be recognized everywhere they go. They'll be standing in line at a fast-food restaurant, and the person behind them will unconsciously be evaluating their order. At the grocery store people will unconsciously analyze what's in their basket. How about the constant nuisance for tall people enduring others unconsciously wondering if they play basketball? There are so many biased thoughts against fat people and tall people it's a wonder they don't just stay home. Maybe they don't give it much thought, or they do but they think people will think what they want to think. Why let that interfere with their happiness or success? Successful fat and tall people are everywhere.

Latino Americans? It should be expected that any new immigrant group faces some amount of discrimination. The Latinos seem to be fairing rather well compared to many other immigrant groups before them, like the Italians and Irish. Household incomes are over $60,000 and this is often an outcome of a single earner. Latinas are the least likely of any female ethnicity to work. Famous Latinos fill Hollywood. Marco Rubio, Ted Cruz, Antonia Novella and Julian Castro are powerful political leaders. Alex Rodriguez in his day was the highest paid baseball player. In 1980, Robert Goizueta started a long tradition of Latinos in senior business positions. This helps to explain the rapidly growing Latino GDP. Latinos have to know that some people think biased thoughts against them. Like other immigrants, lower wages can brand them as job stealers. When they speak, people

---

[vi] America's Jewish population is virtually 100% white.

can unconsciously think Spanglish. Back home, overt discrimination prevented success. Worrying about the possibility of covert discrimination in the form of biased thoughts that don't affect success would be a useless distraction from engaging in opportunities that they never could have back home, just like the Italians, Jews, and Irish before them.

Asian Americans? It seems hard to sympathize with Asian Americans when they complain about discrimination. From education, to wages, to health, Asian Americans outshine every other group. Asians have proven that in America education is the great equalizer and then some. The heads of some of the largest companies in America are run by Asians. That includes Microsoft and Google. Kamala Harris, an Asian and black woman, is Vice President of the United States. Still the Asians are like everyone else; they can face discrimination. When it comes to university admissions, affirmative action blatantly discriminates against Asians. It's a penalty for being too successful. In 1926, Jews became the first groups to face discrimination in college admissions for being too successful.[47] When the pandemic hit, lots of Asians complained of discrimination because all were seen as Chinese and the pandemic originated in Wuhan, China. They complained, but few seemed to get hung up on it. What's the point of getting bogged down in something that somebody may or may not be thinking, or even doing if it matters naught in the whole scheme of things? All that does is suck energy away from being successful.

Native Americans? Indigenous populations are disproportionately in poverty all over the world. The United States more than any other nation has implemented policies and programs to lessen poverty. Still, the nation harbors guilt that is probably unhelpful for Native Americans standing on their own legs. Many Native Americans have, however, let history be history and taken the plunge of merging into mainstream America. They may be Native Americans but what people see is Americans. Many Native Americans are assuming senior positions in national and local governments, Hollywood, professional sports, and commerce.

In seventy-one countries it is illegal to be a homosexual. In America, the forecast is for zero biases against homosexuals between 2025 and 2045. [48] Reasons speculated for the decline are that LGBTQ are well integrated into society, and LGBTQ come in all colors, creeds, and socioeconomic levels, and they work in offices and live in communities everywhere. Additionally, most people have a fond friend or family member that is LGBTQ, or they have familiarity with famous LGBTQs like: US Secretary of Transportation Pete Buttigieg and Chicago Mayor Lori Lightfoot; one of the world's richest women, comedienne Ellen DeGeneres; businessmen Barry Diller and Tim Cook; newscasters Anderson Cooper, Don Lemon, and Rachel Maddow; astronaut Sally Ride; and prominent transexuals like Caitlyn Jenner, Laverne Cox, and Rachel Levine. American LGBTQs are the most successful LGBTQ group in the world.

The priority on addressing discrimination against LGBTQ, and specifically transgenders, was clear in a 2021 presidential executive order that decreed that transgender people could use the bathroom and locker room of their choice and they could play sports per their gender of choice. [vii] Jim Crow laws were written to be race neutral and this order is written to be gender neutral, but the impact is clearly greater on females. Statistics are imprecise, but the number of transgender females is believed to be about four times that for transgender men.

[vii] Some schools, organizations, and states have specific requirements for transgender women competing in women's sports

This order could be a setback for aspiring cisgender women in sports. Additionally, lots of females can find the ladies and locker room uncomfortable but the second sex needs to embrace this as a victory for lessening discrimination for transgender Americans. [49]

There are, however, other implications because school and work policies are being enacted to provide a non-discriminatory environment for transgenders and these in turn can discriminate against a parent's fiduciary duties. In the states of California, Oregon and Washington, for children over 13 or 15 depending on the state, schools can facilitate the provision of puberty blockers and sex hormones without informing parents. Planned Parenthood can do that too. In Oregon, children can have state-sponsored gender reassignment surgeries without informing parents, although it is noted that this is expected to be rare. The California teacher's union supports gender reassignment surgeries without parental consent, but this is still TBD.[50, 51,52,53,54]

The administration of puberty blockers and sex hormones to teens also discriminates against cisgender students because 80-95% of teens suffering through a period of gender dysphoria, will eventually identify with their biological sex. An article in the Economist commenting on the danger of helping students to transition to their non-biological sex concluded that "clinics [schools] should ensure that children in transgender clinics undergo comprehensive mental-health evaluations. For all this to happen there needs to be an acknowledgment of the dangers of starting children on often irreversible treatments. At present, that is unimaginable." [55]

The model transgender policy for Virginia public schools includes helping students to decide on their gender identity without informing parents, reporting parents that are unsupportive of their child's preferred gender identity, and punishing teachers or students who fail to use the preferred pronouns of a transgender person. [56] The latter can be quite tricky because the pronoun list goes beyond he and she to include they, which is for people that identify as gender neutral or nonbinary, but also neopronouns, which include ze, fe and xe. Many teachers to avoid the possibility of using the wrong pronoun and accidentally discriminating against a student based on sexual orientation, ask students to declare their sexual preference, for example, cisgender, genderqueer, nonbinary, lesbian or homosexual, and also their preferred pronoun. One of the challenges for children designating cisgender, is this category is "unprotected" while all the others are protected. This has led children to select one of the protected categories. This can be really confusing to parents when they learn that their child selected nonbinary, etc. to avoid discrimination.

In the real world all sexual orientations are protected, but the reality is no one cares about discrimination against cisgender people. So, the group today facing the most amount of overt discrimination based on sexual orientation are cisgender, but no one cares about that. And no one seems to care that addressing possible discrimination against the 0.3% of the population that are transgender, requires discriminating against female athletes, parents of gender dysphoric children and cisgender children, in addition to making a lot or people uncomfortable in their private spaces.

What about discrimination against Jews? Jews face discrimination all over the world. They have been on the run for centuries because so many people hate them. The Germans hated them so much they decided to intentionally eradicate them. Lots of other ethnicities joined in. Americans were key to ending the Holocaust and throughout history, America has been a key refuge for Jews and nearly half of all Jews live here. Like the Irish, discrimination could be horrible, but still better than where they came from and this includes being targeted by the KKK along with blacks, Catholics, and republicans.

The sympathy for Jews even after WWII has really been in short supply, and discrimination is overt and heinous. Desecration of their temples, asset confiscations, and calls for their elimination are regular. In 2019, National Geographic published an article on French Jews leaving France for Israel because anti-Semitism was reaching new heights. [57] Even in America, anti-Semitism is hardly inconsequential. It is also much more common among blacks and Latinos and it can be overt.[58] A number of black leaders have been vocally anti-Semitic, including Louis Farrakhan, Sharpton, and Jeremiah Wright. They have endeavored to paint Jews as culprits rather than victims. Blacks are the victims. In 2020, Black Lives Matter promoted their anti-Zionist platform and accused the Jews of genocide. BLM supports Marxism and Marxism is anti-Semitic. Also, in 2020, in the midst of the George Floyd protests, African American daytime talk show host Nick Cannon, Jewish-slurred a show on Jewish conspiracy theories. Compelled to apologize after his show was cancelled, he tweeted: "I hurt an entire community and it pained me to my core, I thought it couldn't get any worse. Then I watched my own community turn on me and call me a sell-out for apologizing." Cannon became an Uncle Tom for apologizing to the Jews and to America. African American NFL superstar DeSean Jackson is a veteran kneeler during the national anthem. He also has a foundation committed to social justice. In 2020 he posted this quote *attributed* to Hitler on Instagram. "Because the white Jews knows that the Negroes are the real Children of Israel and to keep Americas secret the Jews will blackmail America. They will extort America, their plan for world domination won't work if the Negroes know who they were. The white citizens of America will be terrified to know that all this time they've been mistreating and discriminating and lynching the Children of Israel." [59,60] The NFL came down swiftly on Jackson, at which point an NBA player, Stephen Jackson, another confirmed social justice advocate, defended DeSean by adding some anti-Semitic remarks of his own.

In the 21st century, anti-Semitic and anti-Zionist discourse has also been found in the halls of Congress from two Democratic Socialist members, Somali American Ilhan Omar and Palestinian American Rashida Tlaib. In 2019, Omar was voted anti-Semite of the year, edging out Louis Farrakhan. It may have been her rationalization of a boycott against Israel by referring to a boycott of the Nazis that pushed her to the top.[61] Then again, Tlaib made the same comparison. Tlaib thinks that merging Jews and Arabs in a common state, which would eliminate a Jewish majority, and hence Jewish sovereignty, would be an equitable solution and deliver social justice to the Palestinians. She said: "There's kind of a calming feeling I always tell folks when I think of the Holocaust, and the tragedy of the Holocaust, and the fact that it was my ancestors, Palestinians, who lost their land…" [62] Tlaib is either very light on history or she has crafted a cunning story for Americans that are light on history.

What is most amazing about this long and continuing history of anti-Semitism and anti-Zionism, is that the Jews are educationally and financially the most successful ethnoreligious group in the world and also in America. Jewish Americans include Ruth Bader Ginsburg and Elena Kagan, Janet Yellen, Stephen Spielberg, Jonas Salk, Armand Hammer, Michael Dell, Safra Katz, Mark Zuckerberg, Cheryl Sandberg, Larry Page, Ben Bernanke, and Alan Greenspan. I could go on and on. You would think that discrimination was so smoldering Jews would live in a deep depression and be afraid to leave their homes.

Just the sight of the Jewish Star of David or a yarmulke can instigate biased thoughts that could be stifling if Jews cared to speculate. But that's not a Jewish obsession. Jews are well aware of the hatred that continues to follow them. No group has been victimized more than the Jews, but they are not allowing victimhood to interfere with being the most successful ethnoreligious group in the world.

How about women? The second sex label for women exudes discrimination, and this has been their history. Four years after slavery was abolished one of the most influential philosophers of the era, John Stuart Mill published The Subjection of Women. He describes white women as living in a state of bondage and having so few rights that they are virtually enslaved by their husbands. He points to women being unable to own property and the inescapability of all the duties of a wife. Mill does note that wives might be treated better than slaves. He wanted the world to know that slaves are not the only ones that face unconscionable levels of discrimination. [63]

All men were given the right to vote in 1870. There ended up being restrictions that disenfranchised many poor white men, and black men disproportionately. Still, for women, the 19th Amendment giving them the right to vote didn't become law until 1920 and there was a ton of opposition. The first affirmative action programs were implemented in 1941. They were for minorities. Women were added in 1961. The inclusion of sex in the 1964 Civil Rights Act was an accident. A Virginia lawmaker added sex to the bill because he felt sure it would kill its passage. One hundred and five years after Mill wrote The Subjection of Women, in 1974, head and master laws that gave a husband sole authority to manage community property was declared unconstitutional. In 1993, spousal rape became illegal across the United States.

The biggest impediment to passage of the Violence Against Women Act (1994) was giving women the same rights as blacks to sue their violent attackers. There is a long history of gender discrimination, glass ceilings, walls, and escalators, and sexual harassment. It's amazing that women haven't given up. Why are they flocking to colleges to get ahead? Don't they know about the unconscious biases that surround them, like men wondering what they are like in bed, speculating if they are menstruating, and wishing they would return to being barefoot and pregnant. Don't they know that depending on the city, people commonly denigrate women on Twitter, but not blacks, Latinos, gays, transexuals or the disabled?[64] Don't they know it will be the 23rd century before there is gender equality? Patriarchal societies have been around forever and there are tons of transitions that have to take place for men and women to experience equality.

Maybe women do know, but they also know that in a relatively short period of time (since 1964), women have reached the top spots in lots of fields. Maybe with the likes of Oprah Winfrey, Hillary Clinton, Condoleezza Rice, Sonia Sotomayor, Amy Coney Barrett, Grace Hopper, Jennifer Lopez, Katherine Johnson, Meg Whitman, Ann Wojcicki, Lisa Su, Nancy Pelosi, Ellen Ochoa, Kamala Harris, and Nikki Haley and hundreds of others as role models, women are powering through the myriad of biased thoughts that see leaders as men and women as homemakers and playthings. No question if women dwelled on what people might be thinking about them, that would be stifling and the 200 years to equality estimate might be 500 like it is in Iran and Pakistan.

America's history included systemic racism against blacks. Fortunately, this is history. Hustlers can denunciate America's health care, criminal justice, and educational systems as racist due to disproportional outcomes, but this doesn't make it true. Opportunistic race baiters can pound the narrative of racist America because they aren't letting whites off the hook, but racist societies don't pick and choose which members to discriminate against within a group. Oprah Winfrey is the richest black woman in the world. Imagine that. There are 50 black majority nations in the world, and the richest black woman comes from the 13.4% minority black population in the United States. Ditto for the two highest paid female athletes in the world, Naomi Osaka and Serena Williams. Five of thirteen black billionaires in the world are American. Nine of the top ten highest paid American athletes are black. African American NFL quarterbacks Russell Wilson and Patrick Mahomes made the list, but not the greatest of all time (GOAT) white Tom Brady, or Aaron Rodgers, or Drew Brees. The most popular athlete in the world is the African American baseball player, Jackie Robinson.

A black man occupied the oval office for two terms. The first time he beat a white war hero with a white woman on his ticket. People still wonder about that white woman. The second time he ran against a white Mormon and another white guy. Some said Romney's religion didn't matter; most know better. There hasn't been an Italian-, Jewish-, Latino- or Asian- American president. There also hasn't been an Italian, Latino, or Jewish vice president. There is a black and Asian vice president, and she is a woman. But there have been no white women in either position. These unrepresented groups in the White House are obviously victims of discrimination, no?

Some question how discrimination against blacks can be in the past when blacks perceive discrimination everywhere. Watch the Starbucks training video on racism.[65] Blacks are afraid to leave their house. They live in fear that someone is going to *think* they are a thief or dangerous, or they think their presence will make people uncomfortable. The video also shows a white guy, and he says he is not afraid to leave his home. He must be ignorant or doesn't care what people think. When people of color or even woke white people see him there is an equal probability that they are thinking he is an arrogant racist as the chance of a black man encountering someone thinking danger.

Michelle Obama fears discrimination too. Michelle graduated from Harvard Law School in 1988. She was the First Lady of the United States from 2009 to 2017. In 2019 she was listed as one of the most 100 influential people in the world. The Obamas are some of the wealthiest people in the United States. She is truly a rags-to-riches story. By 2020, Michelle's memoir sold 14 million copies. In 2020, she addressed the nation at the Democratic National Convention. She said she knew some wouldn't listen to her because she was black. It's hard to conceive of Michelle Obama as another victim of white oppression. But she does have a strong black identity and victimhood is part of that identity.

This identity is a real problem for blacks and America. Victims obsess about past and possible future victimization. They have a perpetual need to have their suffering acknowledged and for the alleged perpetrators to express feelings of guilt. However, there is no forgiveness. There is only revenge. While life is full of ambiguous situations that non-victims seamlessly navigate, victims exaggerate ambiguity and see intentionally harmful actions. Victims see themselves as having high morals and ethics and everyone else as immoral and unethical. The world is composed of saints and sinners. Victims are saints. When victims behave aggressively, they see their behaviors as a rational response to being a victim of oppression, and they will not accept responsibility for the harm inflicted on others. Victims are so enmeshed in their "own suffering" they lack empathy for others that may be suffering because they believe others can't know what real suffering is like.[66] This paragraph may warrant a second read because it sheds light on so much of what is occurring today.

One can hardly blame blacks for obsessing about victimhood. Everyday blacks and all Americans are fed a steady diet of systemically racist America. Turn on the TV, go to social media, and there is another story of a black person that has experienced a slur, an alleged "racist-tinged" accusation, a run in with the law that looks really suspicious – like racist, or being treated disrespectfully by a medical doctor. Or there is a new survey on perceptions of racism or a special on slavery. There is also the tireless work of pimps and hustlers that rely on blacks embracing victimhood for their power. How can blacks *not* feel like victims?

If the mainstream media and social media wanted too, they could make victims of everyone. If woke people expanded their victim horizons, they could hit that cell phone video button to document cross-group encounters among Latinos, Asians, blacks, whites, Native Americans, women and men, people that are right, left, and moderate, fat people, tall people, Jews, Muslims, Christians, and LGBTQ. They could film anything that could be interpreted as disrespectful, or an imbalance of power and then post it to YouTube, and promote it on social media as racist, just like the white girl at Chipotle asking repetitive black diners and dashers to pay for their food. Now, everyone could be victims of white oppression, including whites. Then what? Would everyone be afraid to go outside? Or would everyone face the reality that everyone experiences biases and discriminating is human.

Many would surely be inclined to wonder why people go berserk over things that most people pay no attention too, because in the whole scheme of life they are irrelevant. They might also see that perceptions rarely match reality. If they upped their game to learn what is legal and illegal discrimination, they would find that 99.9999% of what is perceived as discrimination is not illegal, either because it's not discrimination, or it's not illegal discrimination. America's legal system focuses on protecting enumerated rights and freedoms. To do this it cannot get bogged down in human thoughts, speech, and behaviors that do not infringe on these rights. Maybe then people can move on and quit thinking the worst in people. Race relations will dramatically improve, and everyone can return to focusing on having a growth mindset that is so important to achieving a better life than their parents, or even achieving impossible dreams like being president, a famous actor or athlete, or running one of the world's largest corporations. Things that are only possible in anti-racist leader America.

Critical Race Theory Snake Oil

So much of what is said today doesn't make sense. Incessant chants of systemic racism, equity replacing equality of opportunity, extended villages rather than nuclear families, politicians calling capitalism "slavery by another name,"[67] defunding the police while crime soars, BLM activists regularly igniting bedlam in our cities, get out of jail free social-justice cards, politicians gaining legions of followers hawking socialism, intractable political divisions caused by leftist leaders playing the race card, politicians seeing white supremacists in every corner, daily pronouncements of if disproportional then racist, diversity training as key to saving the nation, and centering American history on slavery. It makes even less sense, to find an untested theory underlying all that seems bizarre, except that poverty pimps and race hustlers see the tenets of Critical Race Theory (CRT) as key to amassing and maintaining power.

Introduced in 1989, CRT is anti-American and anti-white. It is a conspiracy theory of whites obsessed with maintaining a superior position in society to ensure the inferiority of non-whites. It has strong ties to Marxism. Instead of class struggles it's concerned with race struggles. [68,69]

CRT is used to predict and explain racism. Explaining and predicting is something all tested theories can do. The problem for CRT is that it's not tested. The problem for America is that it never will be and that's not diminishing applications by pimps and hustlers to opportunistically explain, predict, and most importantly today, to initiate preventive measures to stop the possibility of discriminatory acts.

Biological determinism, more familiarly known as Scientific Racism, was a theory that advanced that racial behaviors are determined by genetics — naturally. CRT takes the nurture side. It takes the position that race is not biologically determined, but rather socially constructed and whites intentionally construct themselves as superior at the expense of people of color. Whites do this to oppress non-whites and leave them powerless. How do whites construct themselves as superior? CRT maintains that the law and legal institutions in white societies are inherently racist and that whites use the institutions of the state to further economic and political interests. They do this specifically at the expense of people of color. This, in turn, perpetuates racial inequality, poverty and criminality in the communities where people of color live. All of these outcomes are then the fault of whites.[70, 71]

Biological determinism was once used to rationalize slavery and the disenfranchisement of women.[viii] CRT's conspiracy theory of a white obsession with superiority is just as outrageous, but while the former continues to send shivers up people's spines and cause whites to cringe with great embarrassment, there is no outrage for CRT and no embarrassment either. Instead, it is celebrated as a truism that supports the endless recitations of white supremacy, white racism, white privilege, and systemic racism. There have been some black and white scholars that have taken serious issue with CRT, but these people are dismissed as racists or Uncle Toms and CRT continues to be accepted as a verified "theory" explaining so-called minority powerlessness, with a focus on black

---

[viii] Around the time of the emergence of biological determinism, Arthur Gobineau took aim at Italians. Italians were cast as a degenerate product of mixed races. In this time period there were many so-called "theorists" and others obsessed with a belief in superiority. This was also a time when Chinese claimed superiority over all races, and Muslims claimed superiority to non-Muslims. Superiority rationalized subordinating populations.

powerlessness. CRT didn't always focus on blacks; this became a later development. It was by necessity because it became obvious that the "theory" was false. CRT was not predicting racism. Asians had become the most educated and prosperous racial group in America, and Latino prosperity surpassed black prosperity. The remedy became to modify the theory. Instead of it predicting racism it would be used to predict white racism against blacks.

Data showing African Americans as extraordinarily and increasingly successful in all walks of life, and the most educated and prosperous black population in the world can be dismissed by the story that whites permit a few blacks to prosper in order to conceal black powerlessness due to white oppression. Stories are crucial to CRT. This is because CRT is a very special theory where stories with morals are valued over empirical research and analysis. Morals are so important to proponents of CRT they take precedence over law – think judicial activism. Latino American Richard Delgado one of the founders of CRT said: "CRT should devote its efforts to critiquing social institutions, legal doctrine and the culture of racism — not itself or its own members." CRT being unconcerned with truth is consistent with progressive views.[72] It is also important to its staying power.

Placing less value on academic rigor is also consistent with black views toward intellectual pursuits. Blacks generally devalue intellectual activities. Look at university enrollments and graduation rates, the number of research publications,[73] scores on high school reading and writing proficiency tests, performance in schools and universities, and scores on standardized tests, like SAT/ACT, MCAT, and LSAT. In all of the above, blacks underperform whites and Asians, and in most cases Latinos. The differences are statistically significant. The list of America's Nobel Laureates is a list that conjures up thoughts of the United Nations, but there is a complete absence of black Nobel Laureates, outside those that have received the Nobel Peace Prize.

African American Columbia University Professor John McWhorter calls anti-intellectualism an unfortunate aspect of black culture. He ties anti-intellectualism to black victimology and a general desire to reject "white culture" and stay different and separate from whites.[74] As you might imagine raising this aspect of black culture has had its critics. The most vocal has been African American Professor Kevin Cokley from Southern Illinois University. His research, however, confirmed it. Cokley found that "African American students are intrinsically highly motivated, this motivation is not related to how they perform academically or their academic self-concept…One possible explanation may be that for many African American students, learning for learning's sake may be seen as a luxury that is not instrumental to doing well in school, getting a job, and making money."[75, 76] Cokely has repeatedly tried to pour cold water on black anti-intellectualism. The problem is that the data supporting it is everywhere.

McWhorter was not the first to draw attention to black anti-intellectualism. In 1992, African American Sophonia Scott Gregory penned the article The Hidden Hurdle. In it she describes how talented black students find one of the most insidious obstacles to achievement comes from their peers. "The anti-achievement ethic championed by some black youngsters declares formal education useless; those who disagree and study hard face isolation, scorn and violence." These were punishments for "acting white."[77]

Research by African American Harvard economist Roland Fryer, and white Northwestern economics Professor David-Austen Smith further supported black anti-intellectualism. In their paper titled *The Economics of Acting White* they reported that "some individuals can receive social benefits large enough to outweigh benefits they might otherwise receive via education and wages. In a purely rational sense, these individuals prefer peer acceptance to the benefits of education." [78,79]

Previously noted, storytelling is key to "validating" CRT. This seems completely logical because proponents are unable or unwilling to seek corroborating data, they can be anti-intellectual, unconcerned with the truth, and they can deprecate objective rational thinking because this is another aspect of acting white. [80] What makes no sense is that this "theory" is pervading the decisions of political and economic decision makers. America is supposed to be all about science. It's not supposed to be taken in by a conspiracy theory that is anti-white and anti-American. African American Michael Javen Fortner, and the author of the Black Silent Majority wrote on July 5, 2020: "Analysis of racism has been transformed from a set of observations and falsifiable propositions into its own epistemology: a way of knowing that bends reality to its will and distorts everything it encounters." Let's have a look at some key CRT tenets.

CRT is against theories of equality, neutral principles of constitutional law, and legal reasoning. A system that delivers equality of opportunity is rejected. To end oppression, CRT maintains that our systems must be built on preferences that deliver racial equity. Instead of equality of opportunity, the goal is equality of outcomes. In 2014 "71% of white families lived in owner-occupied homes, compared to 45% of Latinx families and 42% of black families…racial equity would be if there were relatively equal percentages of all three." [81] In a similar equity vein, CRT calls on the best universities and employers with good jobs to proportionally allocate them without regard for qualifications. They reject merit and objective practices because they are cast as biased and because the bias is in the system it cannot be overcome. [82] In the words of former Harvard Professor Nathan Glazer, they want to shift from a goal of "equality of opportunity to statistical parity." [83]

CRT maintains that the legal system must address unconscious biases. Discriminatory thoughts must be extinguished. These biases are the alleged reason that blacks are underperforming relative to other groups. Blacks prioritize ending biased thoughts that others may have of them, or rather the perceptions of biased thoughts, over economic success, because they believe this is *the* deterrent to success.[84] The late African American Harvard Law Professor Derrick Bell, an originator of CRT wrote, "progress in America's race relations is largely a mirage obscuring the fact that whites continue to consciously and unconsciously, do all in their power to ensure their dominion and maintain control."[85] One has to admit, Professor Bell tells a good story.

America's foundations of democracy and capitalism created a foundation that has given America the most successful minority populations in the world. But CRT finds these foundations problematic. One reason is because America's constitution had a fugitive slave clause. It also permitted the Supreme Court to see a racial component in citizenship in the Dred Scott decision (1857). The 13th (1865) amendment nullified the fugitive slave clause. The 14th amendment (1868) eliminated ambiguity on who could be a citizen, and the 15th Amendment (1870) made sure that newly freed black citizens had a constitutional right to vote. In the second half of the 20th century, there were a range of anti-racist laws passed and implemented. Nice but no cigar. According to CRT, it doesn't matter what America does it can never escape its racist origins.[86] To CRT proponents, the fugitive slave clause proves systemic racism – it's in the foundational documents of our nation.

CRT also has a problem with capitalism. It sees it as a racist system that perpetuates inequality. The rationale that people that work harder, have more experience and seek superior educational outcomes deserve to earn more money is unpersuasive, because some people will be unable to do this -- due to unconscious bias. Capitalism is "slavery by another name." CRT wants skin-color rather than qualifications to fill positions. This may be another reason why CRT has problems with democracy and capitalism. They want discrimination to be legal against some people. The Nazi's wanted something similar and they succeeded. They incorporated Scientific Racism into their legal system. [87]

It's really obvious that CRT's inventors and advocates are like a lot of Americans - light on knowledge of political and economic systems and also global history. The outcomes of the huge live experiments on capitalism's alternative in the Soviet Union, China, Vietnam, and Cuba were obviously missed. The leading proponents of CRT tend to be lawyers, rather than economists, which helps explain why so many positions are deaf to economic logic, but it doesn't explain how a group of lawyers are going to propose and enforce a law to control biased thoughts, but this might. With support of the George Soros Foundation, there have been efforts to persuade American lawmakers to incorporate Behavioral Realism into law. This "realism" would account for the impact of unconscious biases on discriminatory acts. Actually, it can't do this because the relationship between unconscious biases and discriminatory acts is *de minimis*. This raises the question why are CRT advocates placing so much emphasis on biases that have a virtually non-existent impact on people's success? It appears that there is a quest to root out residual racism. This may be an objective as daunting as the search for the holy grail. This is a quest for something that never has been and never will be – not here, not for blacks, whites, Asians, Latinos – and not anywhere – not even Africa where 99% of people are black. There is another big wrinkle to the Behavioral Realism canard. The study used to support Behavioral Realism was retracted, [88] but that doesn't mean that lawyers in support of CRT and social justice won't keep trying to plug an unsupportable theory of Behavioral Realism to support the disproven theory of CRT. [89,90,91,92]

If all else fails, another legal approach to control biased thoughts might be to look at Chinese re-education or the Soviet gulags, but this requires brainwashing techniques, perhaps torture, and a police state. After a lawyer for PBS called for re-education camps for the children of parents that voted for Trump, and numerous politicians and pundits called for reprogramming 74 million voters for Trump, no one can be so daft to think this is ridiculous. [93] Totalitarian ideas are definitely on the table. To tackle racism in the United States, a leading CRT advocate has proposed an anti-racist constitutional amendment "to fix the original sin of racism." [94] (Sometimes the original sin is slavery, other times its racism. It's always hard to keep made-up stories straight.) It would include a "department of anti-racism (DOA) comprised of formally trained experts on racism and no political appointees…[Read this as no one is held accountable.] The DOA would…ensure [policies] won't yield racial inequity…and monitor public officials for expressions of racist ideas. The DOA would be empowered with disciplinary tools to wield over and against policymakers and public officials who do not voluntarily change their racist policies and ideas."[95] This anti-racist amendment would legalize discrimination when it facilitates equity but make it illegal when public officials create solutions to treat all Americans equally. You can see why something like this would require an amendment to the constitution and why this would need to be overseen by "trained experts." The courts couldn't handle the growing body of what constitutes discrimination, because discrimination is not what is defined in the legal system, but rather "whatever any person of color thinks it is."[96] Sounds crazy right, like it could never pass? It truly sounds like a manifestation of George Orwell's 1984 dystopian society, where the government becomes the thought police. The professor that proposed it is Ibram Kendi and he runs the Anti-Racism Center in Washington DC. He is feted by lots of powerful people that are complicit in the narrative of systemically racist America. The same people in government that are implementing discriminatory "equitable" solutions.

It's hard to believe that the creators of CRT could devise a tenet that whites intentionally construct themselves as superior at the expense of people of color with a straight face. There is only one block of nations where race- and ethnicity-based discrimination that affect equality of opportunity is illegal. Further, there is only one block that makes indirect discrimination illegal for the same purpose. These are western (white) nations. Africa and Asia are rife with countries that offer no protections for people of different races or ethnicities, not for direct or indirect discrimination.[97]

Singling out the United States as a white oppressor is not only wrong it is insulting. After 1964, whites, quite unusually in the world, voluntarily relinquished the lock on power they had on institutions. Dominated by white men, a long list of programs, policies, executive orders, and laws were put into place that specifically strive for equal treatment under the law. Since 1965, $23 trillion in government assistance has been disbursed to facilitate equality of opportunity for people with lower incomes. Blacks have been four times more likely to participate in government assistance than whites. Latinos have been three times more likely. The private sector and private philanthropy have been equally generous and supportive.

The very notion of a theory of white oppression and black powerlessness in a nation with a two-term black president, a black female vice president, fifty-seven current black Congress people, 1/3rd of the nation's 100 largest cities having African American mayors, and the face of very successful African Americans in politics, industry, and sports being admired around the world is an absurdity. There is no nation in the world where a minority holds this much power.

The progress of African Americans in the course of a little over fifty years is unprecedented. In 1964 Jim Crow laws were put to rest and in 2009 a black man was president of the United States. A family of four on welfare in the United States has more income than the average family in 90% of the countries of the world. In the words of African American and Hoover Institute Senior Fellow, Shelby Steele: "One of the most remarkable things in all of human history is the degree of moral evolution that white Americans have made from the mid-60s to this day (2006). No group of people in history have morally evolved away from a social evil that quickly and to that degree in this sort of short span of time. And very often, in our calculations in thinking about race, we don't give whites credit for that."[98]

The success of America's multiracial society is globally extraordinary. However, these actions are dismissed by the proponents of CRT. They advance that the reason whites help blacks is for self-interest. It won't be hard to find a story for this one. The renewed incessant attention to slavery, racism, and victimhood makes it simple to find white people harboring guilty feelings about slavery or racism and wanting to assuage that guilt. It could only be in America that people in the 21st century could be made to feel personally guilty for slavery that was abolished in the 19th century, and for systemic racism that was obliterated in the mid 20th century. People feeling guilty for people they didn't know, things they had nothing to do with and never would have supported. Things America has diligently corrected and continues to address with vast amounts of resources. There is no nation in the world that has done so much to remedy an injustice. Indeed, there is no nation that comes remotely close.

Whites in Europe have also shown guilt for a long period of oppressing people of other races. After WWII, some European nations modified very restrictive immigration policies to allow people of all colors and creeds to immigrate from nations where it's very likely they would never experience anything but poverty and repression so they could experience prosperity and freedom. One reason was guilt for centuries of imperialism. Thank goodness for whites in the western world having a guilty conscience. Billions of people are trapped in a subordinate, repressed, impoverished existence all over the world, but the whites and non-whites leading these nations don't feel guilty. Why would they? They have institutionalized discrimination, and that's the way they like it.

The tenets of CRT are regularly refuted in the everyday happenings in America. In this book there are many refutations. Disproving data seems to count for nothing. We are supposed to be a nation that believes in science. Hard data. Now, we are a nation being driven by stories. We are a nation founded on rule of law, but now we substitute personal morals for law, but only for "victims." Instead of justice we have social justice, but only for "victims." Conspiracy theories normally raise eyebrows. Not this one. The leftist purveyors of CRT have a conspiracy theory as ridiculous as the CIA creating HIV to wipe out black people and gays. There is irony that some advocates of CRT like President Obama's spiritual advisor Jeremiah Wright, Ibram Kendi, and Louis Farrakhan support/supported that theory too. [99,100] Farrakhan in 2020 is also peddling in the conspiracy theory that Dr. Anthony Fauci, and Bill and Melinda Gates plan to depopulate the earth through the Covid-19 vaccine.[101]

Whites could do America a world of good by showing the same level of outrage for CRT and its offshoots, as the outrage displayed for biological determinism. Or scoff loudly at yet another absurd conspiracy theory. QAnon is a featherweight compared to CRT. It's time for the people of color to be embarrassed for presenting and perpetuating an immoral and outrageous conspiracy theory. Don't hold your breath because this conspiracy theory supports both the narrative of systemically racist America and the victimization of blacks that is a source of black power. Besides that, no one is taking the purveyors of CRT snake oil to task anymore. Those that have done so, have already been called racists and Uncle Toms. They have already found that the mainstream forces stuffing the narratives of white oppressors and black victims, racist America, systemic racism, white supremacy, and white privilege down people's throats, control the conversation.

CRT is a real problem. It is being taught in universities all over the country. It informs the proliferation of useless to harmful unconscious bias training, politically divides the country, blatantly discriminates against white people, inspires racial unrest, encourages costly benevolently racist practices, glorifies socialism, denigrates democracy, and now it's being indoctrinated into young children, compliments of the New York Times Project 1619. It is a con job spawning more con jobs.

Legal and illegal discrimination

Illegal discrimination. In the 1960s and 1970s, it became illegal to discriminate against people *based on* race, color, religion, sex, national origin, age, disability, and sexual orientation in the areas of employment, housing, pay, and when acquiring financing. The laws focus on tackling discrimination that limits equality of opportunity. In the 1960s and early 1970s, it wasn't hard for the courts or the Equal Employment Opportunity Commission (EEOC) to make a finding of discriminatory practices because discriminatory practices were obvious. At this time, courts often presumed discrimination. With each ruling, human resource departments across the country took action to make sure their employers were in compliance. Soon, blatantly discriminatory practices were uncommon. The law and the courts had eliminated systemic discrimination and there was no longer a presumption of discrimination. [102]

How can the legal system see an end to systemic discrimination in employment, housing, pay, and when acquiring financing, while chants of systemic discrimination are deafening? That's easy. There are no legal doctrines that accept the original sin of slavery or racism, or the overturned fugitive slave clause as indicative of systemic racism. Further no legal doctrines support unconscious biases as an impediment to equality of opportunity.

Discrimination in employment is where most allegations of discrimination arise, and more often than not the allegations don't meet the test of being illegally discriminatory. The law protects people from discrimination *based on* race, color, religion, sex, national origin, age, disability, and sexual orientation. If someone is fired, for example, because they are insubordinate, they disrupt a company meeting by starting to pray, or they use company resources to contact relatives in a foreign country, they are not afforded extra protections that others do not have should they be in a protected class. This is because their termination was not due to their race, color, religion, sex, national origin, age, disability, or sexual orientation. There are though many more qualifications to qualify as legally discriminatory. An employment action must also meet the reasonable person test for being intimidating, hostile, abusive, pervasive, or severe, [ix] and it must result in an adverse action, such as a failure to be hired or get a pay raise, a termination, or quitting because the workplace is hostile or dangerous. How often are adverse actions tied to discrimination? Not very often. The most common reason people aren't hired is they are unqualified or not the most qualified. Most people that are involuntarily terminated were unsatisfactory performers or engaged in any number of inappropriate behaviors, like stealing company property, or insubordination.[103]

Qualifications. Anytime a profession isn't divided 13.4% for blacks, 18.5% for Latinos, and 1.2% for Native Americans, that seems proof enough to make a claim of racism. It's the "Racist Law of Disproportionality," but it's not the law or even a law and it does not prove discrimination. Players in the NBA are 81.7% black. In the NFL, 70% of players are black. Is that due to racism, or because blacks are better qualified? Qualifications explain disproportionate ratios for most professions.

[ix] "The reasonable person standard aims to avoid the potential for parties to claim they suffered harassment when most people would not find such instances offensive if they themselves were the subject of such acts." Society for Human Resource Management.

It used to be that the courts could make a finding of discrimination if it could be statistically proven that an employer clearly had a preference for people of certain races or genders. This is much less so today because it has been found that it is impossible to statistically prove that disparate outcomes are due to race, or gender, or some other protected class. There are just too many qualitative factors. [104] For example, just because an employer has hired Asian Americans for 38 out of 100 software development positions, this doesn't mean the employer discriminates against non-Asians. Asians are most likely to major in engineering and computer sciences. They are only 5.7% of the population but they occupy 38-39% of hardware and software development positions. Why are Latinos disproportionately present in the trades? Because they study the trades, and this is often on-the-job-training. In carpentry and masonry Latinos occupy 37- 68% of these positions. Blacks are disproportionately present in positions in the social sciences and that's because this is where blacks are most likely to major. It is why blacks occupy 20-30% of positions in community services. They are also most likely to major in technical health care degrees and this explains why they occupy 20-40% of positions as home health aides, and licensed practical nurses.[105]

Education affects who gets hired for what positions, how much they are paid, and the likelihood that they will stay employed longer. Many jobs require a four-year degree. Thirty-five percent of whites have a bachelor's degree or higher. For Asians, it is 54%, blacks 21%, and Latinos 15%. [106] Having a high school diploma is often required because it is an indicator that a candidate will have basic skills, like communicating effectively, being organized, exercising self-control, being able to grasp new concepts, time management, and handling money. More and more people are graduating from high school, but there are still too many that are missing this basic qualification for employment. According to the National Center for Education Statistics, in 2018 Latino dropouts were 8.0%, blacks 6.4%, whites 4.2%, Asians 1.9%, and Native Americans 9.5%.[107] It's not discrimination if a person isn't hired because they lacked requisite qualifications.

It's also not discrimination if people aren't hired because they don't apply for a job. In 2021, the issue of racism in baseball was raised because African Americans represented 8% of Major League Baseball (MLB) players. Could this be a result of racism? Forty years earlier, in 1981, blacks were 18.7% of MLB players when blacks were 12% of the population. As the population of African Americans fell in the MLB, the population of black Latinos from Latam grew. In 2017, Latinos were 27.4% of MLB players and most were black. Independent researchers looking into why more African Americans weren't playing baseball found a lack of interest in the sport. Some said it was boring and too slow. Others said they preferred basketball and football. The rise in black NBA players is supportive. From just 2015 to 2020 the roster of black players rose from 74.3% to 81.7%. It's not racist if the NBA is 81.7% black, and it's not racist if the MLB is 8% black.

Perceptions of discrimination does not equal discrimination. Perceptions of illegal employment-related discrimination are pervasive. In some cases, perceptions don't reflect discrimination, and in other cases the perceptions may reflect something discriminatory but not illegally discriminatory. Fifty-six percent of blacks say they have faced discrimination at work that led to adverse actions.[108] That would amount to about 500,000 claims per year assuming one claim per black person in their work lifetime.

It's pretty common for terminated employees to threaten to sue their employer for discrimination. But few do. A big reason for this is that the EEOC must validate that there is probable cause before a discrimination lawsuit can proceed. Claimants are asked to provide concrete examples – not perceptions of discrimination -- and to validate the adverse action. The intake questionnaire alone, can cause many would be sue-ers to end the initiative.

Between 1997 and 2019 (22 years) there were 680,000 claims of racial discrimination. That's a lot fewer than the 9 million possible claims just noted. The EEOC found no issue with 64.3% of the claims. Another 18.3% were closed for administrative reasons, and 4.8% later withdrew the charges. Those that took their claims to court had to prove that the alleged discriminatory actions were hostile, abusive, pervasive, or severe. If their company had a policy for addressing perceptions or overt discrimination, they also had to prove they adhered to it. [109] In the end, a tiny fraction of a percent of people that perceived discrimination prevailed as victims of illegal discrimination. Similar outcomes exist for gender discrimination claims. Most of these have been filed by white women.

So much press has been devoted to pervasive racism and sexism it seems reasonable that people would reflexively think they are the reasons for an adverse action. Most often, they are not.

The role of employers in addressing discrimination. It's common in the United States for organizations to play a larger role than the government in addressing different issues, such as social issues or environmental issues, because they find them to be in their economic interest. It's an incredibly powerful aspect of capitalist systems. In the case of discrimination, organizations don't want to miss out on hiring the most productive candidates for any reason. In 2003, a study was done that showed a resume with the names Jamal or Lakisha would get fewer calls for interviews than John or Suzy.[110] This ignited the use of blind resumes where a person's name and picture were removed. The use of blind resumes was probably not as important as raising an awareness to the possibility that people were passing over the best candidates because of a name. Studies show today that people have been giving preferences to resumes with ethnic or female sounding names. A study in Australia in 2017 found when people saw names on resumes that they thought were for minorities or women; they gave them a preference. When the resumes were blinded, these preferences went away. [111] In a series of studies with ostensibly biased people in the United States in 2016, people gave a preference to candidates they thought were black.[112] A similar study with similar outcomes was conducted in 2001. Managers that were apparently biased against black people, were more likely to hire blacks.[113] In a 2020 study using identical resumes in the United States, Malik Washington was favored for an interview over Christopher Wu, William Schmitt, and Jose Vasquez. Just as relevant there were no names that generated a strong bias.[114] When the nation arrives at a point where positive discrimination overtakes negative discrimination, it's time to take a victory lap. The Chapter: Unconscious Bias and the Lie of Systemic Racism, covers another significant something organizations are doing to try to address perceptions of, or overt discrimination.

Illegal discrimination deficiencies. With or without the additional measures taken by American employers to address discrimination, advocates of social justice find the policies of human resource departments and anti-discrimination laws deficient. These advocates have sought a way to administer justice for any and all allegations of discrimination. To do this, the constitutionally protected right to be innocent until proven guilty has had to be trampled on.

It was the time of #MeToo. Scores of women published allegations of sexual harassment on social media. Women were naming names. It became so popular; it took on the feeling of an open season on men. Without the benefit of a trial, judge, or jury, men were being convicted of being sexual predators or at least sexist pigs in a court of public opinion. To protect themselves from accusations, an increasing number of male colleagues and bosses began consciously and unconsciously avoiding one-on-ones with females, and many still do.

Helen Lewis, the author of Difficult Women: The History of Feminism in 11 Fights thinks the lingering unhelpful #MeToo outcomes are a result of the slogan Believe All Women. It was a recipe for allegations that were exaggerated and even false. There is a similar situation with racism today. Every day there is a new crop of articles and accusations alleging racism. Many are exaggerated or false. White America and Americans with some frequencies are being wrongly convicted in a court of public opinion. A person that tries to defend themself or the nation is silenced by a chorus of systemic racism, white supremacy, and white privilege. Racism today is like the number 42 in the Hitchhikers Guide to the Galaxy. It's become the answer to everything.[115] In the workplace, it's closer to the answer to nothing. The probability of racism in the workplace is infinitely less than sexism. Sexism is incredibly common and generally accepted by men and women, racism is not. Call a woman a whore and people laugh; a white person calling a black person brother or sister can find their career over as they are dragged through a court of public opinion that casts them as a racist spewing racial slurs.

In 2020, Digiday ran a story about the lingering impact of #MeToo in the advertising industry. Male and female workers are segregated. Male clients work with male workers and females with females.[116] Can you imagine if an outcome of the uncontestable racist accusations against whites led to workplace segregation between whites and blacks? Or blacks and whites avoiding one another. It certainly wouldn't be out of human character for people to try to protect themselves, in this case by seeking the comfort of like people. Since whites are more often in a position to help blacks than vice versa, much like men are more often in a position to help women, this would be a terrible outcome.

Pay discrimination. On average about 1,000 claims are made for pay discrimination annually. About 22% are found valid.[117] The reason there are so few pay discrimination claims and far fewer successful claims is that pay discrimination is virtually non-existent. That may surprise some because there are regular reminders that women only make 80% of men and blacks make 83% of whites. The implication is that it is due to sexism or racism respectively. Pay disparities are commonly presented absent the context of qualifying data. Differences in hours worked, qualifications, experience, seniority of position, choice of profession, and locations of employment explains most or all of the differences. Look at the difference just location makes. The states with the highest average pay, those in the northeast and west, have average pay that is 75% higher than those in the deep south.

Much of the disparity in pay among racial groups ties very closely to levels of education and occupation choices. Black and Latino college completion rates have been 38% and 45% respectively. For Asians and whites, it has been 63% and 62% respectively. College enrollment rates for blacks and Latinos are also lower. The difference between blacks and Asians is 39 points. A college dropout makes about 11% more than a high school graduate. A person with a bachelor's degree, on average, makes 50% more than a dropout.[118,119] When it comes to occupation choices, according to the Bureau of Labor and Statistics, average annual pay for hardware and software developers is $95,000-$100,000. For carpentry and masonry, it is $55,000-$60,000. Home health aides average $26,000-$28,000, licensed practical nurses $48,500, and community service workers $50,000-$60,000. What determines occupational salaries? Skills, education, supply and demand, and how much wealth/productivity is generated by an occupation.

Consider a report that headlined: female STEM workers on average make 34% less than men, and blacks make 29% less than whites. When the level of the STEM degree, degree specialty, preference for private or non-profit employment, and years of experience were accounted for the difference shrank to 4-8% depending on whether professionals had a bachelor, masters, or Ph.D. degree.[120] The analysis did not assess location of employment, and whether people worked 40 hours per week or more than forty. It also did not account for performance or productivity. These areas could easily account for most of what was left and even more. Pay differentials based on any of the criteria just noted are legal.

In many or most corporations there is no pay difference between like qualified males and females of any color because they are diligent in matching pay to qualifications.[121] It is the law – an anti-racist law and it is working.

Social media mob justice. It's pretty clear that people say and do things all the time that are perceived as discriminatory, but legally they are not. The government isn't there to police behaviors that don't have adverse consequences and certainly not to police perceptions of unconscious thoughts or anything considered free speech. This very adult approach is consistent with our protected freedoms and widely held belief in personal responsibility. However, many people have apparently abandoned a sense of personal responsibility, and most people are clueless on what is illegally and legally discriminatory and what is not. They are similarly clueless on what freedom of speech, freedom of the press, slander, and libel mean. For example, just because a white person tells some black men that have dined-and-dashed before that they have to pay for their food, that's neither racist, illegal, or white oppression. [122] But an uploaded video clip of something like this can be interpreted by millions of people as racist, oppressive and illegal. Naturally, this would not hold up in a court of law, but that doesn't change the fact that in a NY second a person's life can be ruined by social media mob rule.

The government takes an adult approach, but social media is frenetic. It has found enormous power in mob rule. Mob rule calls out the behaviors of racists, or at least what the mob thinks is racist. There is a mission to root out anyone that utters something that could be construed as a slur or behaves in a manner that could be interpreted as a slight, and not just in the present. Any non-black person that has behaved in the past in a manner that is consistent with the very high standards the mob has set today for non-racist behaviors, can be subject to mob rule.

Social justice advocates on social media libelously destroy people's lives every day. It's triggered by something or maybe nothing that might be related to discrimination. This mob rule shares resemblances to the Salem Witch Trials and an American version of the Red Guard.

The proper technical term when a social media mob takes a story about a possible, even remotely possible racist act and then turns the target person into a disgusting racist, is called ambient digital racism. [123] That term sounds quite harmless. It's just people having libelous fun destroying someone's life. It's not just social media. The mainstream media does it too. Some have asked why are we primed for outrage at anything that could be racist? Remember Nick Sandman? A white, male, Catholic kid in a MAGA hat at a Right to Life rally. He had to be a racist, right? [124] At least Sandman was able to successfully sue the libelous media. So far social justice advocates libelously destroying someone as a racist on social media hasn't brought much in the way of justice for the libeled. No surprise that the mobs remain primed for some more ambient digital racism and more innocent people will find their lives turned upside down by libelous accusations made by the newly woke.

Much of what people perceive as discrimination is not illegal discrimination and often not discrimination at all. Overt discrimination virtually disappeared nearly half a century ago because the legal system, combined with public and private sector human resource (HR) departments, and decades of attention by America and Americans to ensuring equality of opportunity in their increasingly multiracial society, were doing their jobs. Emphasis has shifted to stamping out unconscious discrimination. This is not something the legal system is equipped to handle. HR departments have again taken the lead in trying to address unconscious biases. This is covered in the next two chapters.

Unconscious bias and the lie of systemic racism

Unconscious bias, sometimes called implicit bias and second-generation bias,[x] influences the attitudes and behaviors of everyone every day. A person walking down a dark street can duck into an alcove when hearing footsteps. Better to avoid the chance of an unpleasant encounter than offend a neighbor out for a walk. A female domestic violence survivor can cower when a man raises his voice. Again, for the same reason. Unconscious biases help people to quickly assess situations with limited information. There are times when quick assessments can be wrong. This is particularly true when they are based on inaccurate stereotypes of groups of people. For example, women are stereotyped as weak and emotional, blacks are dangerous and unambitious, Asians are arrogant and shy, Latinos are unambitious and can't speak English, and whites are arrogant and racist.

Stereotypes don't come from thin air. Women do cry four times as often as men. Thirty-three percent of black men have felony records. [125] A third of Latinos struggle with English proficiency and nearly two- thirds of Asians are self-reportedly shy.[126,xi] Still, if one were to assume that all women are emotional, all blacks are dangerous, all Asians shy, or all Latinos speak Spanglish, a lot of people would face unconscious biases for something inapplicable. If that were to happen, it would turn out that this is okay, because people are not locked into unconscious biases. As their brains process a situation, the biases are supplanted by reality. For example, unconsciously seeing a woman as weak fades when she strides purposefully across the room. Biased thoughts end when data proves them wrong. It happens seamlessly, unconsciously, and naturally because stereotypes are generally wrong.

The terms unconscious and implicit biases are used more commonly than second-generation bias, although the latter carries useful information. First-generation biases are overt and exclusionary. Job requirements that excluded people based on race, gender, age, sexual orientation, disability, and national origin; and unequal pay for people performing the same job at the same level, are examples of first-generation biases. These forms of discrimination became illegal in the Civil Rights Act of 1964 and subsequent amendments. In the first ten years following the Act, these forms of discrimination became increasingly rare. It was evident, however that discrimination still existed, but it commonly took an unconscious form. These unconscious biases became labeled second-generation biases. Unlike the first-generation, the second are next to impossible to pin down from the perspective of managing them through legislation.[127] How could legislation do this? Up to 90% of biased beliefs surface without any forethought (unconsciously). [128] These beliefs appear normal and are consistent with experiences, how people were raised, educated, and socially indoctrinated.[129] It turns out that being unable to regulate unconscious biases is OK because, today, they rarely result in discriminatory actions. Organizations have been very responsive to remedying second-generation biases by altering policies and practices. Additionally, America and Americans have changed a lot since 1964.

This hasn't slowed down the narrative of unconscious bias as the root cause of systemic racism. Narrative purveyors often hang their hats on faulty data, like data from the Implicit Association Test (IAT) and surveys that inquire about perceptions of bias being mistaken

---

[x] Purists can argue nuanced differences in the terms.

[xi] There is no data supporting whites as racists or arrogant. Whites do dominate leaderships in government and business, and arrogance has been seen as possibly influential to success.

for actual bias. Right now, perceptions of bias are off the charts and for good reason. The incessant chants of systemic racism have some groups perceiving bias as soon as they walk out their front doors. The repetition of hearing systemic racism influences the minds of susceptible people and perceptions can and have skyrocketed. Add to this that perceptions of bias are more common among people that believe they are doomed to discrimination, populations with histories of discrimination, those that believe they are surrounded by racists, and those that have experienced or perceived discrimination. Further, perceptions can be influenced by a strong identification with an ingroup. African Americans more than any other racial group find the identity of their race extremely important.[130, 131] A strong black identity is seen as healthy and identifying with another group is seen as unhealthy.[132] Blacks are glorified, and whites denigrated.[133] A strong black identity associates with victimhood. This alone has been noted as a significant deterrent to blacks advancing.[134] This strong identification really increases the chance that perceptions will diverge from reality, but they can be embraced and defended as reality. They can affect psychological development.[135] "For members of disadvantaged groups, attributions to prejudice are likely to be internal, stable, uncontrollable, and convey widespread exclusion and devaluation of one's group." [136] There is another downside of having a strong in-group identity. It has been shown to be a significant generator of unconscious bias against others outside the group.[137] In this case, we would expect blacks to have significant unconscious biases, particularly against whites. This might seem shocking to some because the narrative of systemic racism carries the absurd notion that blacks can't be racists, and this has taken hold. African American Supreme Court Justice Clarence Thomas said identity with race can be both good and problematic.[138] It would seem problematic when the identity includes victimhood. It would also seem problematic in a nation that has endeavored for more than sixty years to create the most successful multiracial society in the world to denigrate the white majority.

How wrong are perceptions of discrimination? Psychologist Daniel Kahneman received the 2002 Nobel Prize for economics for identifying the existence of cognitive biases. These are ways that humans create subjective social realities that are at odds with objective reality. These subjective realities are perceptions.[139] They are distorted realities that can inspire responses that others might define as irrational and having no basis in reality. When it comes to discrimination, this is a big problem and made bigger because perceptions of discrimination feed more perceptions of discrimination. A young non-white person that perceives bias due to her race can inadvertently create a foundation for regularly perceiving discrimination throughout life. That can be debilitating. Anyone obsessing with perceptions of racism, would find it near impossible not to be drained.

In an October 2020 poll conducted by the Kaiser Family Foundation (KFF), 71% of blacks said they have experienced unconscious biases that have resulted in biased actions that created major obstacles in their lives.[140] It seems improbable because biases result in discriminatory actions about 4% of the time.[141] Some think 4% is high, but much of this pertains to discriminatory acts conveyed through body language, such as someone rolling their eyes, shrugging, or standing in a defensive posture. Discriminatory acts that stem from unconscious bias could also include decisions like a Latino choosing to donate to a charity in Argentina rather than Somalia, or a black person choosing to donate to a charity in Somalia rather than Argentina. [142] Even with such a low percentage of biased thoughts translating into discriminatory actions, one might say, well blacks experience a lot of unconscious bias. It would be more correct to say that blacks perceive a lot of unconscious biases since few have the ability to read minds, or even body language.

What is really improbable is that 70% of blacks surveyed, perceived unconscious biases by whites as purposeful in the last 12 months. These 12 months covered most of the 2020 year of the pandemic. Were white people really taking the time to analyze masked-up people to see the color of their skin? Then once having determined they were black, intentionally thinking biased thoughts that created major life obstacles for them. There are two problems here. The accusation is ridiculous and there is the reality that unconscious biases are inadvertent and by definition not intentional.

This survey seemed to infer that blacks see whites as conspiring against them. A belief in this conspiracy is echoed by the African American leader of the Implicit Bias Network, Chris Bridges. He said, "in the outwardly, obviously racist society that we currently live in, implicit bias sometimes operates as the glue that holds that system together." [143] It would appear that CRT advocates are everywhere. CRT, the KFF survey, and the leader of the Implicit Bias Network support a black obsession with racism. There seems to be a belief that whites revolve their lives around discriminating against blacks. What seems more reasonable from the data is that blacks have an obsession with whites. That would be a reasonable outcome from a well-fed conspiracy theory.

Is it any wonder that blacks have become despondent about opportunities in America? In 2011, 65% of black men and 61% of black women thought it was a good time to be black in America. Since the steady chants of racist America that began with the rise of Black Lives Matter in 2013, these beliefs have plummeted. In 2020, it was 20% and 13% respectively. No question perceptions of discrimination are on a tear and it's not having good outcomes for African Americans.

How did we get here? It's really hard to contest the rapid progress blacks and other minorities have made in America. People can point to perceptions, and innuendos substantiated solely by the Racist Law of Disproportionality, but not much more. We are being told there is a reason for that. You can't see systemic racism because it's invisible. It takes the form of unconscious biases. The white human mind is contaminated with biased thoughts, and it is the new enemy number one in the war on racism.

One test more than any other has contributed to the unchecked accusations of (unconsciously) systemically racist America. The Implicit Association Test (IAT) measures implicit biases. Actually, it doesn't, but this became a widely held belief. A belief supported by the now widely repudiated claim in 1998 that "the pervasiveness of prejudice, affecting 90 to 95 percent of people, was demonstrated today in a Seattle press conference at the University of Washington by psychologists who developed a new tool that measures the unconscious roots of prejudice." [144]

The IAT tests have been taken over twenty million times. About 75% of test takers for the skin-color test score "biases" against people with darker skin.[145] (The same percentage was found for "biases" against women.) The Obama White House highlighted the IAT as a measure of implicit biases from people that were "unwilling or unable to report it." [146] Members of the administration became a bully pulpit for unconscious bias, and so did television and radio commentators. Dozens of writers for popular presses concluded that racism (and sexism) is everywhere, and America wasn't making progress; it was a hell hole of racism.

It turns out that the IAT skin-color test does not measure discrimination; it measures preferences. The preference someone has for the company of people that have light skin or dark skin. It turns out more people, on a slightly declining basis are more comfortable with light-skinned people. But then again at least 75% of the people that have taken the test are light skinned. About 50% of blacks were also found to have a preference for light skinned people. [147,148,149,150] In the United States the preference for light skinned people was not very strong compared to other nations. It ranked 94th out of 146 countries. Its preference was the weakest of all light-skinned majority countries in the world except Andorra and Albania. [151]

People preferring to be with someone that is light- or dark-skinned is hardly a measure of racism. And lots of people preferring to be with like people is not a measure of systemic racism. Studies abound that show people like to be with like people, and very importantly this does not correlate with racial hostility or racism.[152] Do these preferences result in discriminatory acts? Rarely. Even the researchers that developed the IAT now admit there is a very weak correlation between the unconscious preferences measured by the IAT score and discriminatory behaviors. [153,154] This sharply contrasts with the positions the researchers widely promulgated just 14 years earlier. Then they said they established that black disadvantage was caused by white people preferring light-skinned people.[155] In a research paper exploring the history of the IAT by professors from the universities of Virginia and Pennsylvania, the professors said, it's "difficult to find a psychological construct that is so popular yet so misunderstood and lacking in theoretical and practical payoff." [156] Then again, popular ideas that are continually promoted, particularly by authoritative sources, like the White House, are often mistaken for the truth. The damage, in this case is incalculable.

The junk claims of the IAT may have been stopped in their tracks if the researchers had bothered to test their assertions. The claims of the IAT have not been found to be a valid or reliable measure of anything. To the contrary the IAT has failed tests for validity and reliability. [157] Now that the IAT has been repudiated, it is hard to get the genie back in the bottle. For example, on January 1, 2021, California introduced a new law that allows the courts to decide if a juror should be excused because there is a "substantial likelihood" that a person has unconscious biases against someone based on race, ethnicity, gender, gender identity, sexual orientation, national origin, or religious affiliation. I suspect the courts will now have a court bailiff and a court mind reader. Watching how this plays out will be entertaining, hopefully not in the form of a tragicomedy.[158]

For twenty years people have been brainwashed by prominent people to believe that everyone is a secret racist. They have been so successful; the retractions can't match the publicity of the false claims. This shouldn't detract from the reality that unconscious bias as the source of systemic racism is another hoax, just like the original sin of slavery and a constitution that has an overturned fugitive slave clause. Still, that isn't stopping the narrative that unconscious bias is enemy number one in the war on racism.

Unconscious bias training. In 2020 the government issued an order to cancel training programs that encouraged racism and sex stereotyping. Seems like a sensible order for a country that has turned all eyes to stopping alleged racism. Not so. The onslaught of criticism was extraordinary. People were crowing that to end systemic racism we had to extinguish unconscious racial biases and the best way to do this was bias/diversity/racial sensitivity training. If the media was doing its job, it would have shown that these indignant social justice advocates were very uninformed when it came to what these types of trainings do and don't do. The media though wasn't doing its job. The research and many experts available to help inform their viewers and readers weren't called upon.

"The positive effects of diversity training rarely last beyond a day or two, and a number of studies suggest that it can activate bias or spark a backlash." [159] "Someone who is prejudiced against women or African Americans before taking diversity training may experience a positive shift in attitudes and become less prejudiced. Yet, their attitudes can shift back closer to what they were pre-training in response to media reports or personal encounters with women crying, or blacks committing crimes." [160] The media is less likely to report an emotional woman than it is to report crime. In the summer of 2020, there were 557 riots involving BLM activists. An estimated $2 billion in damage was done.[161] In 2020, homicide rates are up in many major cities across the country. Most of the victims and criminals are black. Unconscious bias training cannot get people to stop stereotyping blacks as dangerous. Only black behaviors can do that.

If people actually thought through a decision on unconscious bias training, they would know it's tantamount to wishing on a star. Training programs last hours, days or possibly a week. A temporary change in beliefs can happen, but this could not possibly alter a "thumbprint in our brains" reinforced for years and decades, particularly if stereotypes are still being reinforced.[162,163]

For most, unconscious bias training is a waste of time and money and that is a relatively good outcome. An analysis of 482 studies by researchers at the University of Arkansas "found little evidence that implicit bias can be changed long term, and even less evidence that such changes lead to changes in behavior." [164] Worse, unconscious bias training can be counterproductive and increase bias. Some people can find the training offensive because they see themselves being singled out as prejudiced. Remember although most people prefer light-skinned people to dark-skinned, most people are supportive of light- and dark-skinned people. Biases can also increase because the training creates an us vs. them scenario, or because people in their efforts to suppress seeing women as less competent or blacks as less ambitious, now can't help but see women as inept and blacks as loafers. [165,166,167]

A more pernicious outcome of these types of training is that it can perpetuate racial subordination. Training can include advising people not to put too much value on someone's ability to write, or the ability to substantiate positions with data. People can be cautioned to avoid talking about minorities as having less education or achievement, and also to refrain from thinking that all people embrace hard work, rational thought, and careful planning as personal values.

For white people the training is difficult to stomach. It is racist. Diverse people often sit in a room, and they are taught that whites are different. They are privileged, and oppressors and they should feel guilty. Whites are shameful. Whites busy worrying about the safety of their children, aging parents, health concerns and paying bills, just like blacks, Asians and Latinos, are being trained that they must focus on ending oppression particularly against blacks because it has made them powerless. They are also trained to see that treating people equally is wrong. Blacks, in particular need to be treated special. Whites can be urged to dig into their unconscious to unearth unconsciously biased thoughts and then confess. If they can't come up with anything they are urged to think harder. Should a white person only think admirable thoughts about blacks he or she can be told they are in denial. They suffer from white fragility, and this certifies that they are racists. You can see for some middle-class white person trying to keep his family above water, this training is all very confusing.[168]

It wasn't pre-1964 but the summer of 2020 when Seattle hosted segregated unconscious bias training sessions. There was one session for whites and one for BIPOC. The training for whites centered on dead and gone white supremacy. It was called Internalized Racial Superiority. The content: "We'll examine our complicity in the system of white supremacy . . . and begin to cultivate practices that enable us to interrupt racism in ways that are accountable to Black, Indigenous and People of Color (BIPOC)." The likeness to the struggle sessions in the Chinese Cultural Revolution where people were forced to humiliate themselves in front of others is undeniable. In these sessions, confessions were not optional. They only thing missing in this American version of struggle sessions is using physical torture to compel confessions. An organizational psychologist commenting on the training said that this was typical content for these types of training. [169]

Did America really need so many studies to conclude that this training can be counterproductive? Think about it. People go through life treating everyone equally, now they are being trained that they are serial discriminators. There is no evidence of discrimination; their crime is biased thoughts. It sounds positively Catholic. White Americans are being relentlessly hammered with non-stop chants of systemic racism. The problem is that the world's leading anti-racist nation cannot do more to enforce and encourage equal treatment before the law. Add to this that the heavy lifting of addressing how unconscious biases can affect decisions related to equality of opportunity has been done. All that is left of racism is residual, and it too shall pass. It will though take longer if the media, schools, corporate training departments, and politicians remain fixated on wrongly accusing America and white people of systemic racism. [xii, 170]

In October 2020 a black British MP Kemi Badenoch took to the floor in Parliament and called for training programs in government and schools that taught white privilege and instill white guilt for something that their ancestors may or may not have done as regressive and racist. Of course, she is right. Hopefully, this will be another episode where per Winston Churchill, Americans can be counted on "to do the right thing after they have tried everything else." The problem is that America has already done and continues to do the right thing. The data is already overwhelming.

Has our nation become imprisoned by poverty pimps and race hustlers peddling stories of victimhood and demanding that one ounce of bias against blacks must be extinguished with brainwashing? Why? Political power? That is why the Chinese engage in brainwashing.

[xii] Consistent with Project 1619, children as young as 3rd graders have been asked "to deconstruct their racial identities and rank themselves according to their "power and privilege."

Benevolent Racism and Sexism

Benevolent sexists have a positive view of women. They see them as wonderful but weak, and in need of being taken care of. Benevolent sexists think when they call a woman honey or shield a woman from a job with more responsibilities that they are being nice or protective rather than patronizing. The female recipient can feel the same way. Women that are receptive to the behaviors of benevolent sexists encourage more of the same.[171] Two German researchers, Julia Becker and Steven Wright, found women that view benevolent sexism as appealing and nice, were more likely to see the value in perpetuating the status quo of subordination.[172]

The impact of benevolent sexists and sexism is similar to that from benevolent racists and racism. Benevolently racist people are sympathetic to people of color, but they see them as incapable. Benevolently racist practices "presumably help, empower, or protect communities of color [but] can often support and reinforce— either deliberately or inadvertently—a system of racial domination." Benevolent sexism inadvertently or intentionally keeps women subordinated and benevolent racism inadvertently or intentionally keeps people of color subordinated.[173] Benevolent racism is like benevolent sexism in another way. People of color can be receptive and encourage these behaviors. This self-perpetuates subordination.

In America we have many benevolently racist programs and laws including the War on Poverty Programs, affirmative action, and minimum wage laws. There are also benevolently racist narratives, like systemic racism.

War on Poverty Programs. War on Poverty programs are hailed for facilitating a level playing field between blacks and whites. This omits the reality that blacks had been doing quite well without these programs. In the 1940s, the poverty rate for blacks was 87%. In 1960 it was 47%.[174] Sixty years later, it is 20.8%. This is in spite of about $1.1 trillion annually in government assistance, or is it because of? In 2012, 13.2% of white Americans, 42% of blacks, and 36% of Latinos received public assistance.[175] The largest *median* monthly payments went to blacks. This was $446 versus $410 for Latinos and $366 for whites. These payments don't include the costs of what are called non-cash benefits. This includes, for example, food stamps, housing subsidies, and Medicaid. The maximum annual value of welfare benefits that a recipient can receive varies by state. In 2013 the range was $16,984 in Mississippi to $49,175 in Hawaii.[176] At current spend levels the cost to taxpayers is on average $16,176 a year for each of 68 million welfare beneficiaries. Most recipients have been short term, or less than 12 months. Long-term recipients are considered dependent and so are people that receive more than 50% of their income from the state. Blacks are 40% more likely to be dependent than Latinos and four times more likely than whites. The people most likely to be long-term recipients live in poverty, are single-parent female-headed households, children,[xiii] high-school dropouts, and unemployed. Latinos have a shrinking edge on high-school dropouts, but otherwise the blacks lead in all categories.[177] Single-parent female-headed households were 878% more likely to be dependent than married couples.[178]

Early on government assistance programs were framed as social safety nets that were designed to tide people over a rough patch. In the 1970s they were recast as entitlements.

[xiii] According to the National Center for Education Statistics 34% of blacks and Native American *children* live in poverty, 28% of Latinos, and 11% of whites and Asians.

Not short-term entitlements, just entitlements. The notion of being on welfare used to motivate people to get off of welfare. Then welfare became an entitlement. Long-term programs that offer what recipients see as a satisfactory existence facilitates dependency (addiction). When it motivates people not to work, there is the slippery slope of increased crime, and also an inability to find work. It is much easier to get a new job when someone already has a job.

Before the War on Poverty programs, 22% of African American households were single parent, black crime was low, blacks moved for better opportunities and they knew education was the great equalizer.

"The welfare state has done to black Americans what slavery could not have done, Jim Crow and the harshest racism could not have done: namely destroy the American family." [179] George Mason African American Professor Walter Williams, 2015.

"The welfare state … substitute[d] a check for a father, a social worker for a caring mother or grandmother, and a slew of civil rights organizations for the neighborhood church." [180] African American Kay C. James, president of the Heritage Foundation, 2018.

It would be hard to forget then candidate Obama's Father's Day speech of 2008. "Children who grow up without a father are five times more likely to live in poverty and commit crime; nine times more likely to drop out of school, and twenty times more likely to end up in prison."

Black rapper Bill Stephney rapped about the ill effects of welfare: "Marriage will knock out the child-industrial complex she can enjoy, which can include AFDC, health benefits for her children, housing and energy assistance programs, day care, off-the books employment…We have the money-for nothing welfare mentality."

War on Poverty programs also curtailed motivations for people to move for better opportunities. During the Great Migrations (1910-1970) millions of blacks moved from the south to other parts of the country where opportunities were better. Today, this curtailment is widely felt, and it's unlikely to change. "Even at the height of the civil rights era, socializing with whites was never a goal in itself for black people, and undoubtedly for many, it is not one today." [181] That's an unfortunate outcome. Networking with white and Asian neighbors, and black children having the friendship of white and Asian kids that prioritize their studies could open up access to opportunities beyond what's possible in black communities. The same would be true of Latino children and Latino communities.

Affirmative action. Affirmative action programs give an advantage to select groups, and blacks have benefitted more than others. Or have they? When people with lesser but still high qualifications are merged with those with higher qualifications, the former can't keep up. For example, when top schools lower SAT admission requirements by 100-150 points for minority candidates, these students often have trouble keeping up with other students, commonly Asians or whites, that met the requirements. Sometimes these students will change majors to programs that are less academically demanding, they drop out, or they suffer mentally from performance that is inferior to their classmates. In some cases, students don't keep up because they carry the stigma of being a token or somehow unequal, rather than someone that attained their position based on merit. This is true even when they would have attained a position based on merit. Blacks and Latinos are generally assumed to have been accepted based on diversity goals rather than academics. [182,183] In 1996 Stanford University ended its affirmative action program because they saw affirmative action as promoting discrimination.[184]

When goals for diversity take precedence over excellence, the system is corrupted. Minority students that may have excelled and felt great about their accomplishments at a good university where their high-school grades and SAT scores met requirements, can feel like failures or inferior students at a top school. Meanwhile, the schools can tout that their universities mirror the population.

The data on outcomes of affirmative action-type programs is plentiful, but universities have been fighting hard to maintain them because there is a priority on demonstrating student body diversity. When courts have struck down programs as discriminatory, colleges find work arounds like altering SAT scores with adversity scores or eliminating SAT and ACT scores all together. No question, diversity appeals to stakeholders. Failed programs can be censored or massaged, for example, by showing that affirmative action students graduated with good grades while withholding data on students changing majors, for example from a STEM program to humanities. Meanwhile, blacks and Latinos that could have been leaders in their fields and communities can suffer the ill effects of being foist into learning environments for which they are unprepared.[185] Affirmative action programs are benevolently but inadvertently reinforcing racial dominance.

Minimum wage laws. Another benevolently racist practice is minimum wage laws. Walter Williams said, "A lot of people think minimum wage is an anti-poverty device. That doesn't pass the smell test." Policy makers have benevolent intentions when they support increases in the minimum wage, but they dismiss the discriminatory effects these laws have on lower skilled people. These people don't get the higher wages, because they don't get hired. Lower skilled people would be more likely to be hired for a lower wage that fairly compensates them for what they are able to produce. Then they could gain experience and skills that would ultimately qualify them for a higher wage. The people that suffer the most from minimum wage laws are young blacks and Latinos that lack experience and have lower educational attainment.

Before passage of the Minimum Wages Act of 1948, black teens had a lower unemployment rate than white teens. It was less than 10%. Young blacks were a more cost-effective choice. Once minimum wages were set, whites were found to be more cost effective, and unemployment rose for blacks. Minimum wage laws, however, hurt all youths for the same reason; they don't have the skills to justify the wages. Still, they hurt blacks and Latinos more. In the summer of 2020 youth unemployment (16-24 years of age) was 16.7% for whites, 25.4% for blacks and 21.7% for Latinos. When unemployment is long term there is an increase in violent crime, which increases rates of detention and incarceration. Minimum wage laws also have other unsavory effects. The National Bureau of Economic Research has shown that property crimes increase when minimum wages increase, because lower-skilled people cannot find work. The research did not specifically address increases by race, but black juveniles make up 41% of arrests for property crimes. [186,187,188,189]

Other. In 2020/2021 programs were being devised for select groups. In 2020 Oregon created a Covid-relief fund for black Oregonians. The fund sent a message to struggling

Latino, white, and Asian owned businesses that they could figure it out, but blacks would struggle to do this. Many programs that are specific to blacks send a similar message: blacks need extra help. (A lawsuit has been filed alleging that this program is unconstitutional.)

Reviving slavery. Why are politicians and other leaders regularly reminding blacks that their great ancestors may have been slaves? Refreshing a history of black slavery reminds blacks of a time when their ancestors were victims. It reminds them of a period of white racial dominance. The refresh is working. Eighty-four percent of blacks say that slavery affects them a great deal or a fair amount. [190] Most whites, Latinos, and Asians don't know who their great ancestors were, or if they were free or unfree. Millions of white Americans taking ancestry tests have discovered that they are black and also descended from slaves. The effect? A likely first thought is wondering if they could get admitted into Harvard or Yale with lower test scores. A second might be wondering if they could be eligible for any reparations. [xiv,191] Can you imagine if the up to 80% of the world with ancestors that were enslaved or worse, dwelled on this? They would think they were inferior and incapable of a better life. Better to let distant memories or possibilities stay distant than to regularly revive them. Anything that perpetuates victimhood is benevolently racist.

Systemic racism. In the summer of 2020, there was a vigorous revival of a pre-1964 diagnosis on race in America and it caught on like wildfire. It was impossible to turn on the TV without hearing systemic, structural, or institutional racism five times in the course of an hour. (The words are synonyms.) Millions searched online for the meanings of structural, systemic, and institutional racism. They didn't find the original sin of slavery or racism, the overturned fugitive slave clause, or unconscious bias, although the latter may have been inferred. What they found is that systemic racism is racism baked into society. For proof they found charts and data that reflected the Racists Law of Disproportionality (if disproportional then racist). What was left out of the data were the underlying reasons for disproportional outcomes that had nothing to do with racism. For example, disproportional outcomes in health care correlating to the attention or inattention given to diet and exercise, and disproportional outcomes in education correlating to attention or inattention to studying. This data pointed to self-inflicted problems – not systemic racist problems. [192]

The unsubstantiated systemic racism narrative has been repeated so many times; many have embraced it as true. In an October 2020 survey, blacks identified structural racism as the biggest obstacle to racial equality. Education, housing, and job opportunities fell to the bottom of the list.[193] Systemic/structural racism that had existed in the first half of the 20th century was being reimagined in unconscious biases. Blacks were inadvertently saying they could not solve problems of disproportionate presence and success in some areas without the help of whites. There was nothing blacks could do because they believed, or at least said, it was in the system. Blacks had a lot of help coming to this conclusion. Powerful politicians, professional athletes, journalists and commentators surely knew, or they should have known that the correlation between biased thoughts and discriminatory actions is extremely weak, and that disproportionate racial/ethnic outcomes are not pre-

---

[xiv] The United States is unique in not distinguishing between blacks and mulattos. In the United States people with "one drop" of black blood have been considered black, although this is changing. People are increasingly likely to self-identify as mixed race.

ordained by something in America's systems. If the desired outcome is to have blacks increase their perceptions of unconscious biases to a point where they find them so oppressive, they have become the biggest obstacle to superior outcomes, it worked. It is indeed a big obstacle. How does someone surmount an illusory impediment? Add to this, the insanity for a population that is generally culturally averse to all things white, including white people, looking for whites as their solution. This is a request for racial dominance. This is a recipe for non-blacks moving forward while blacks tread water or regress.

For blacks and others addicted to government assistance, it can be hard to see the downsides that would lead to objecting to programs that deliver so many dividends. Who doesn't like to go to the head of the line or receive free stuff? Besides, for blacks, the prevailing belief is that whites owe us. Per the false narrative, whites owe blacks because America is systemically racist, because of slavery, and because whites are born racists. Why would people that are given preferences, and cash transfer programs that facilitate dependence (addiction), question that special treatment rather than helping people to succeed, cements an image of blacks and to a continually diminishing degree Latinos as disproportionately and unnecessarily dependent, incapable, victims, that need extra help when others do not?

People that encourage dependencies are perpetuating a form of modern slavery. Leftist policies taking their cues from poverty pimps and race hustlers look like the work of drug dealers feeding the addicted.

Never in the history of the United States has so much attention to helping one racial/ethnic group been given. Before the Great Society people had to learn to be self-reliant, hard-working and observe the rule of law. Blacks started out that way too. Then democratic lawmakers oversaw the passage of the components of a welfare state, a system of preferences and social justice programs that would lessen the drive to become more educated, to get married, to be employed, obey the rule of law, and take risks to have a life better than their parents. These programs have made millions of blacks and Latinos dependent on the government. African American Harvard Professor Glenn Loury said, "no people can be genuinely free… so long as they look to others for their deliverance."[194]

> "The worst enemy that the Negro have is this white man that runs around here drooling at the mouth professing to love Negros and calling himself a liberal…
> If the Negro wasn't taken, tricked or deceived by the white liberal, then Negros would get together and solve our own problems." Malcom X, 1963.

Remember Frederick Douglas's speech in 1865 asking whites to give blacks a chance to stand on their own legs, and if they can't then let them fall?[195] Douglas was asking for the same chance afforded to every other immigrant group in America. Douglas is, of course, not a leader of blacks today. Black leaders, the ones Walter Williams calls poverty pimps and race hustlers either have a quid pro quo relationship with leftist politicians or they are leftist politicians. Blacks trade a voting block for richer welfare programs, preferences, and disproportionately favorable policies.[xv] It is in the interest of all participating parties to "enact programs that sustain and enhance dependency."[196] Leftist

---

[xv] The majority of Latinos vote Democrat, but they are not a unified block. Latinos are also less likely to be dependent on welfare, have an aversion to acting white, or believe that whites owe them. How could they? Most Latinos self-categorize as white. Latinos also do not have a culture of victimology.

politicians garner the support of leftist non-black voters with the guilt-provoking charade of systemic racism while regularly refreshing reminders of slavery and Jim Crow. Most blacks would never admit that the addiction to free stuff and preferences is the source of black fragility. A fragility that will keep blacks subordinated. A fragility that prevents blacks from standing on their own legs. These poverty pimps and race hustlers are causing incalculable harm to blacks and they are trying to do the same with Latinos.

THE POVERTY PIMPS' POEM

Let us celebrate the poor,
Let us hawk them door to door.
There's a market for their pain,
Votes and glory and money to gain.
Let us celebrate the poor.[197,198,]

How does the genie get back in the bottle? Blacks and to a lesser extent Latinos need to end a reliance on a system of benevolently racist programs that inadvertently create dependence and reinforce subordination. Where are the leaders promoting solutions to unemployment, education, good health habits, and two parent families? Where are the leaders that will facilitate a growth mindset rather than killing it by emphasizing victimhood? Where are the leaders that will promote positive racial relations rather than poisoning them with bogus chants of born and bred racist whites? Where are the leaders that will say systemic racism is gone and it's time to move on? Where are the leaders that remind blacks that the most prosperous and educated black population is in America and it didn't happen because Americans are racists? Where are the leaders who will say quit pointing the finger at whites as racists, and look within? Where are the leaders that put an end to the poverty pimps and race hustlers?

Prioritizing politics and race over education

The state of America's educational system is a regular topic. It's not the entire system; private schools get high marks and so do most charter schools. It's the non-charter public schools. This is where many schools get failing grades, particularly in the inner cities.

The inner cities are where charter schools have had some of their grandest wins. Charter schools represent 7% of the public schools in the United States and education to 12% of black students. Most students at charter schools are black or Latino and poor. Not all charter schools have been successful, but the results from some are jaw dropping. For example, the 14,000 students enrolled in New York's Success Academy in 2017 outperformed students at all public schools in the state in English and math. Children that attend charter schools also have higher high school graduation rates and higher percentages of college enrollment. A study from Florida and Illinois found that charter school graduates go on to earn 12% more than students from public schools. Children in DC charter schools had proficiency rates in math and English that were 2 and 3 times higher than black children in non-charter public schools. [199] A study by Stanford University found that in charter schools, "poor black students gained 59 days of additional learning in math and 44 additional days in reading. Latino students with English Language Learning status gained an additional 72 days in math and 79 days in reading." [200] Charter schools are seen as an important component to tackling income inequality. [201] Some black and Latino parents are diligent about making sure their children have a chance to be enrolled because it can be the difference between a child having a successful future or not.

The success of charter schools, however, is a problem for America's powerful teachers' unions (American Federation of Teachers (AFT) and the National Education Association (NEA)) because charter teachers are non-unionized. This means charter schools are a problem for Democratic lawmakers, the NAACP, and black leaders like Al Sharpton and his National Action Network (NAN) that receive financial donations from the unions. It also means they are a problem for their close ally and partner, Black Lives Matter. In the 2018-2019 school year, the unions donated more than $20 million to facilitate electing Democrats. The amount for Republicans was negligible. For the NAACP and NAN the amounts are in hundreds of thousands, but the donation feeder system from Black Lives Matter is counted in millions. [202,203,204] In 2016 and 2017 the NAACP called for a moratorium on charter schools. In 2017 the unions and the NAACP tried to stop charter schools by presenting their disproportionate black and Latino populations as vehicles to re-segregate schools. To kill the charter schools; they implied they were racist. [205] In a bid to help the unions, NAACP board member and the former head of an NEA affiliate, African American Hazel Dukes, accused parents that send their kids to charter schools of "doing the business of slave masters." [206] The NAACP using the race card against black parents desperate for a better education sounds insane, but money and power make people behave irrationally. It seems more reasonable that they would use the race card against white Americans. That is something the teachers' unions do as primary distribution outlets for Project 1619.[207,208,209,210,211]

There is no question that more charter schools, particularly in inner cities, could really be helpful. The black populations in Baltimore, Philadelphia, Detroit, and Washington D.C. ranges from 24% to 82%. In 2016, in 48% of Baltimore's high schools from 0-1% of students were proficient in math. Nineteen percent of 8th graders in Philadelphia were proficient in math, and 16% in reading. In Detroit the percentages were 4% proficient in math and 7% in reading. [212] In Washington DC 28% of black students were proficient in English and 21% in math.[213] The unions' alignment with Black Lives Matter makes sure that these kids are learning that black lives matter, even if it's not evident in the quality of their education. If their dad isn't around, they are learning that's because nuclear families are part of white culture. [214] With curriculums tied to Project 1619 they are also learning if they flunk out and end up in prison, it's not their fault and not their teachers either. Then again, being a school failure can be rewarded with social acceptance for refusing to act white.

What happened to promoting Dr. Martin Luther King's belief that "nothing in all the world is more dangerous than sincere ignorance and conscientious stupidity?" Are the lives of black and Latino school children being sacrificed for political and organizational power and money? It seems this is less true for Latino children. The states with the largest number of charter schools are California, Florida and Texas. They also have the largest population of Latinos. The greater prevalence of charter schools as a contributing factor to Latino students pulling ahead of black students in educational outcomes cannot be ruled out.

President Obama accepted the wrath of the unions and supported charter schools, but many Democrats today will not. Since Obama left office, many blue states are restricting the expansion of charter schools. [215] The mainstream media carries their water by cherry picking data on charter schools to highlight the relative few that have not performed well, and they highlight the need to focus on the public school greater good.[216] The basic rationale is why not instead focus on fixing the public school system that accounts for 93% of publicly funded schools. That sounds benevolent, but America has had and continues to have one of the highest public school spends per student in the world. The solution is not money. Charter schools actually prove that money isn't the problem; they operate at 64% of the per-student spend of public schools. Besides not all public schools are horrible. The worst tends to be serving minority and poor white students. The very students that attend charter schools when given the chance.

It seems odd that some poor kids are being denied a better education by the unions. "The kids don't belong to the unions. The unions are supposed to be working for the kids and not the other way around." The teachers are supposed to be working for the taxpayers that pay their salaries, but the unions have a monopoly on public school education, and they are calling the shots with lawmakers. [217] Unions and lawmakers might be even more successful limiting charters, but there are a number of white billionaires that are determined to give minority and poor white children the chance for a better education. Some of the biggest contributors are the foundations of Bill and Melinda Gates, Ely and Edythe Broad, the Waltons, the Zuckerbergs, and the Dells. [218]

During the pandemic, Al Sharpton called the state of education a five-alarm fire. [219] He was right and the grandest fires were in the non-charter public schools. Unlike private and charter schools these schools and teachers really had problems adapting to distance learning. The hardest hit were minority students. In Seattle, a true champion of social justice, they devised a benevolent solution to the unequal education students were receiving in public schools, non-charter public schools, and private schools. Students in public schools all got As. Outcomes included further decreases in student and teacher participation. What's the point of studying or grading papers if everyone gets an A.

Across the country, when schools began reopening, those with the strongest unions stayed closed longer. [220] Studies that showed no difference or even improved outcomes in virus transmissibility rates when schools were open had no impact on a decision to open. Increases in teenage suicide had little impact. Arizona, West Virginia. Wisconsin, Texas, and North Carolina all reported increases in teen suicides. Some described the rates as skyrocketing. The CDC reported a 24% increase in teen ER mental health visits. Remote learning that deprives children of a social life is the culprit. In 2021 teachers in one school district in Nevada agreed to return to the classroom after 18 students committed suicide in 2020.[221,222] Increases in sexual violence and other child abuse against "home-schooled" children also had no impact. Neither did a record number of women leaving the workforce when the new school year started because it was too hard to work and manage their children's education. The union mantra of one [union] teacher dying kept schools closed. Masks, shields, plexiglass, and sanitizer were not sufficient protection. The Chicago school district invested $100 million into making schools safer, but the unions wouldn't budge until teachers were vaccinated, even though the CDC was relentless in advising teachers that it was not necessary.[223]

How is it that teachers in the classroom were not considered essential? Building buildings is essential, but not building minds. Parents were pleading to get their children back in school, but President Biden was supportive of the union's definition of teacher safety. Candidate Biden in a September 2020 interview with the NEA assured them of his support. Biden also made it clear he was not supportive of charter schools and denounced former Secretary of Education Betsy DeVos's strong support for charter schools and school choice.[224] Union donations to democratic candidates in 2020 is counted in tens of millions. [225] No candidate received greater contributions from the unions, than Biden. [226]

At least kids learning remotely at charter schools found a level of education that was superior to those in non-charter public schools. One big reason is that these non-unionized teachers were more empowered to make decisions and had greater flexibility to operate under extraordinary conditions. They came up with ways to minimize the distance in distance learning. Unfettered by union pressures, charter schools were also more likely to open earlier than other public schools for in-classroom learning either full time or on a hybrid basis. [227, 228] If only there weren't so many powerful interested parties against expanding the availability of charter schools.

The pandemic really demonstrated the power of political donations and the teachers' unions. Preventing a very low probability of any teacher contracting the virus and dying from Covid and some other union posturing was validated as more important than school children committing suicide, and a generation of students with a substandard education. America may soon find that it has a Chinese version of the lost generation. Unlike China's lost undereducated generation, it will be children from lower income families that find life quite a bit harder moving forward because educationally they are too far behind to catch their peers.

It's hard to grasp how it can be possible that the teachers' unions invested about $20 million into political coffers in 2019 and 2020, and politicians returned the favor by supporting the continuation of substandard educations to millions of minority and poor white children. After the pandemic, the unions will continue to do the same by denying poor children an education in charter schools that can provide a superior foundation for a better life. Ironically, this has all been occurring under the so-called benevolent intention of benefitting the greater good.

Education is only the great equalizer when people have equal access to a good education, and students are equally motivated to learn. This points to another problem. Whether it's a black cultural system that deprecates education or one that is okay with students making economic decisions to prioritize social acceptance over an education, this cultural system, in opposition to the school system, has an equal or greater impact on educational outcomes for blacks.

"The phrase "acting white" has often been the insult of choice used by blacks against those [blacks] who moved forward…Today it rejects all the iconography of white middle-class life: a good job, a nice home, conservative clothes and a college degree… Promising black students are ridiculed for speaking standard English, showing an interest in ballet or theater, having white friends or joining activities other than sports…The anti-achievement ethic championed by some black youngsters declares formal education useless; those who disagree and study hard face isolation, scorn and violence." [229] For black teens, doing well in school is a ticket to having fewer friends. [230]

A leading thinker on race in America, African American Jason Riley said, "the black underclass continues to face challenges, but they have to do with values and habits, not oppression from a manifestly unjust society. Blacks have become their own worst enemy." [231] One of the most damning ways blacks have become enemies of themselves is placing more value on peer acceptance, which mandates not acting white. This means, *inter alia,* devaluing education. In this regard blacks are also averse to acting Asian and Latino. Latinos have now surpassed blacks on college campuses. In 2010 blacks outnumbered Latinos, but now Latinos are 19.5% of the student population, blacks are 9.6%, whites 55.5%, and Asians and Pacific Islanders 10%. [232,233,xvi]

Black children might be able to persevere past the peer pressure to dismiss their studies if their parents were education advocates. A study by Clifton Casteel in 1997 found 8th and 9th graders that were white tended to say they did their homework for their parents. Black students were more likely to say they did their homework for their teachers. [234] The influence of parents on educational outcomes can be enormous and far greater than a teacher. Parents influence and often determine if a child goes to school, does their homework, and where they attend school. In order to get into charter schools, mothers or fathers have to be advocates of education that care enough about the education of their child to have them included as a possible student. The value that mom places on education can be especially influential.

More than the school a student attends, the factor that most influences educational outcomes is diligence studying and doing homework. In one large scale study covering high schoolers between 2003-2009 it was found that Asian students spent 13 hours per week studying and doing homework, whites 5.6, Latinos 4.6, and blacks 3.4. At 17.6 hours per week, black children spent the most time watching TV, followed by Latinos with 15.6 hours. Blacks and Latinos similarly spent the most time on YouTube.[235,xvii] Whites spent the most time doing chores (5.9 hours) and also worked the largest number of hours

---

xvi College enrollment for the Fall of 2020 were down for all racial groups by 10% or more. Latinos and blacks had the highest decreases. Reasons include lack of in-person classroom training, minimal student activities, and issues related to Covid-19.

xvii Black parents were found to be least concerned about what their children might be exposed to on the internet. Latinos were the most concerned.

outside the home (5.8 hours). The greatest influencer on children's priorities after school was the attention of mothers and environments that encouraged higher educational outcomes. A large-scale study in 2014 had similar findings on the importance of studying to school outcomes.[236]

Study time influences SAT scores. In 2019 average combined SAT scores for reading and writing were 1223 for Asians, 1123 for whites, 990 for Latinos, and 946 for blacks. This influences admissions to different colleges, although an emphasis on diversity can lessen the impact of lower SAT scores for minorities, and whites from single parent households and areas with high crime. Some schools have rationalized double standards for acceptable SAT scores by pointing to the impact of poverty. Data showing students from the poorest families scoring higher than those from wealthier black families has tested that *assumption*.[237] Perhaps these poor students had moms that went an extra mile to encourage studies and homework.

Once admitted to a university, performance will again be influenced by study patterns developed as children. In college, Asians were again the most diligent with studies. Asians studied and did homework a little over 15 hours per week, whites just over 10 hours, Latinos 8 hours, and blacks just over 7.[238] Studying and graduation rates also correlate. Blacks and Latinos have college completion rates that are 38% and 45% respectively. For Asians and whites, it has been 63% and 62% respectively.[239,240]

The "benevolently oriented" teachers' unions and crony politicians are denying millions of minority and poor white children a superior education. This is doing irreparable harm to America. Improved educational outcomes lead to superior earnings, higher self-esteem, and generally a higher quality of life. These improved outcomes have also repeatedly been shown to be a force for rejecting negative stereotypes and embracing egalitarianism.[241] This latter benefit assumes that schools aren't teaching negative stereotypes, like white racists, and black subordinates, per Project 1619.

Among the biggest challenges that black and Latino children face is that a combination of politics, school and home environments are preventing education from being the great equalizer. Diminished educational outcomes more than any other factor drives inequality of outcomes by race. Pointing a finger at racism is disingenuous, and it is the work of political opportunists, poverty pimps and race hustlers so obsessed with power they are lessening the possibilities for millions of children to have a better life.

Bastardizing History – Project 1619

Parents play a huge role in the success of their children's education and so do teachers. Teachers can motivate children to see in education the chance for a better life. They can also demotivate them by making them think they are inferior, a victim, or of bad character. Teachers can make students proud to be American or teach them to despise America. Why would anyone want to demotivate children or make them despise their country? That's a good question that really needs an answer right now, because that is the path of education in America.

The NY Times- and Pulitzer Center-sponsored Project 1619 has revised American history to make slavery the new centerpiece. This seems analogous to the Germans placing the holocaust where 15-20 million died in concentration camps as the center of their history. Or Saudi Arabia focusing on the Arab slave trade where 20–200 million non-Muslims were enslaved, [242] or centering Nigerian history on the pivotal role of Africans in the African, Atlantic and Arab slave trades. To stay consistent with the NY Times approach, these nations would then need to exaggerate what actually occurred.

Imagine if Germany decided to center their history on the Holocaust and anti-Semitism, instead of teaching these subjects as part of their history courses in high school. Following the path of Project 1619 their founding would be changed from 1871 to 1933 to coincide with the election of Adolph Hitler. Their history would be Jewish-centric. Germans would be taught that they are born Jew haters and they are responsible for everything bad that has and will happen to the Jews. They will be taught that Germans are permanently stained with the original sin of Nazi death camps. They will also learn about German medical experiments on live subjects that involved torture, mutilation and sterilization, and they will learn that their one-time orientation toward biological determinism can never be forgiven or forgotten. They would not learn that 70% of Israelis have an excellent opinion of Germans, who have tried to remedy the acts of their ancestors. This is because that would distract from the narrative of Germans as inherently evil people.[243]

Project 1619 tries to present itself innocently enough. They just want to give black history more prominence. That's what Project 1776 does too. For 1619 it's quite a bit more than that. There is a central theme of black victims and white oppression and the lesson plans indicate a definite revenge objective. That is consistent with people that are obsessed with victimhood. There is no forgiveness, only revenge. This revised history also alters a Eurocentric approach to Afrocentric, or at least African American-Afrocentric. With the financial heft of the Pulitzer Center, the influence of a national newspaper of record and support of the most powerful teachers' unions, at last count, more than 4,500 schools have adopted Project 1619.

Consistent with critical race theory (CRT), the revised history is presented as a collection of stories. If it wasn't for the reality that Americans find history uninteresting, it would seem impossible that the Project 1619 narrative could be embraced as true by so many Americans, including teachers all over the country. But we must be realistic. Teacher certifications rarely rely on knowledge of history,[244] and the unions supply ample materials for teaching their interpretation of social justice, the positions of Black Lives Matter, and Project 1619. It makes sense that so many teachers would want to participate in something they thought could help blacks. It also makes tragic sense that history-light teachers could fill the minds of our children with falsities that will result in many horrible unintended consequences like demotivated children and hatred of America.

Leading historians of the slavery period in America have objected strongly to the false narrative, but objections have been sidelined, downplayed, and ignored. The "brains" behind Project 1619, journalist African American Nikole Hannah-Jones, calls these historians "old, white male historians" unworthy of the respect afforded them. Her comment is both racist and anti-intellectual. These old white men have authoritatively pointed to over 100 falsities, exaggerations, outright lies, salient omissions, and the complete absence of context.[245,246,247,248,249,250,xviii]

The year 1619 was chosen for the Project because it is the year slavery began in America. Actually, that's not when it began. In 1619, blacks were indentured servants just like a much larger number of whites who couldn't afford passage across the Atlantic. When they completed their indenture blacks and whites were given freedom dues which could include land. This accurate historical version of the year 1619 in the Thirteen Colonies can't be taught. For slavery to be central to American history, it must be in the year of "our true founding" in Jamestown in 1619. Project 1619 is determined to show that "anti-black racism runs in the very DNA of this country." [251] Pushing up the date 50- or 60-years messes with the DNA metaphor. The so-called original sin of slavery must have happened in the beginning to solidify the DNA angle and the plot that racism is in America's systems and people from birth.

Here is the banner headline introducing Project 1619:

> "What if, however, we were to tell you that *this fact,* [July 4, 1776] *which is taught in our schools and unanimously celebrated every Fourth of July, is wrong, and that the country's true birth date...*was in late August of 1619?"

In the "country's true birth date" of August 1619 America was a new colony of Britain and some British privateers hijacked a ship heading to Mexico. Then they delivered 20-30 black indentured servants who joined a larger bunch of white indentured servants, who also arrived in 1619. So, 1619 wasn't the year when black slaves first came to America. Was it the first year that black men came to America? No. At least one black conquistador, Juan Garrido, arrived in Florida in 1513. He later became an owner of black slaves in Mexico.[252] That's probably not the slavery DNA that Project 1619 was angling for.

When Hannah-Jones, was questioned about the "true birth" she replied that anyone should have known that she was speaking metaphorically. Got that schools kids? When you read that, it's a metaphor, or maybe as Hannah-Jones said, anyone should know that.

In selecting the stories to use, Project 1619 could have chosen to tell stories about blacks that owned or sold slaves in America. These stories would help with the problem of missing context, but these are story spoilers for the theme of white oppression and black victims. They are though perfect for an Afrocentric approach to history. About 25% of free blacks in the south owned slaves.[253] In 1860 about 4.6% of southern whites and 1.25% of

---

the US population owned slaves. [254] Specific examples of blacks that owned or sold black slaves include, Anthony and Mary Johnson purchased John Castor, a black indentured servant in 1654 for life. Normally indenture didn't exceed 20 years. Blacks didn't have to indenture blacks they could purchase the indenture of whites in this time period. Nat Butler was a slave trader. Andrew Durnford, a physician and plantation owner with 77 slaves, admitted that self-interest was stronger than any desire to free his slaves in the 1800s. Some black slave owners were avid supporters of the confederacy fighting to perpetuate slavery. "The free colored population [native] of Louisiana … own slaves, and they are dearly attached to their native land … and they are ready to shed their blood for her defense. They have no sympathy for abolitionism; no love for the North, but they have plenty for Louisiana … They will fight for her in 1861 as they fought [to defend New Orleans from the British] in 1814-1815." If the Project had selected these stories, it could lessen the impact by arguing that black slave owners were benevolent (so were some white slave holders). The problem is some were not benevolent. Even black slave owners that were considered benevolent for buying wives, engaged in selling their wives and children.[255] Imagine the pain of a black person today that has bought into the white oppression story discovering that his ancestors owned slaves, or he was owned as a slave by a free black person, and these ancestors or owners acted like oppressive white people.

The choice of 1619 is curious for another reason. Our nation was founded in 1776, and it is our founding that Hannah-Jones tells one of the more damning lies.

> "In other words, we may never have revolted against Britain if the founders had not understood that slavery empowered them to do so; nor if they had not believed that independence was required in order to ensure that slavery would continue…some might argue that this nation was founded not as a democracy but as a slavocracy."

The response by historians to this assertion was vigorous and lengthy, including our nation was founded with a rejection of the old-world theories of superior races and supreme rulers.[256] The feedback was so intense, Hannah-Jones did respond: "I should have been more careful with how I wrote that," because I don't think that any other *fact* would have given people the *fodder* that this has. [257] It's a good thing that this "fact" was thoroughly debunked to show slavery had nothing to do with the American Revolutionary War. The "fact" though persists in the materials the Pulitzer Center has supplied and continues to supply to educators. In one exercise, students are asked to answer how "some might argue that this nation was founded not as a democracy but as a slavocracy?"

Hopefully, the perpetuation of this "fact" won't lead to another round of what Hannah-Jones dubbed the summer of 1619 riots, this time calling for Juneteenth to replace the Fourth of July for America's real day of independence.[xix] Defeating the British Empire would be out, and freeing slaves in Galveston Texas would be in. The National Anthem would be out, and Lift Every Voice and Sing would be in. These possible alterations would be consistent with centering American history on slavery.

George Washington is also out, or at least thoroughly discredited. Project 1619 teaches that "enslavers dominated the federal government, Supreme Court and the Senate from

---

[xix] Juneteenth reflects a day that Union troops arrived too free slaves in Galveston, Texas following Texas ratifying the 13th amendment.

1787 to 1860." [xx],[258] Great Americans are reduced to enslavers. Students are taught that America was a nation of enslavers, even the fearless explorers were enslavers. Columbus was not looking for silks and spices; he was motivated by slavery and so was Ponce De Leon. Enslaver is often used as a synonym for American – white American.

NY Times Magazine Editor, Jake Silverstein showed that he also had a gift for sensationalizing history. "Out of slavery — and the anti-Black racism it required — grew nearly everything that has truly made America exceptional." It just seems like British, Irish, German, Italian, Jewish and other immigrants that faced incredible struggles to survive and prosper did some things that helped to make America exceptional. For the record, the vast majority didn't have slaves. Having a slave required money and most Americans were poor, many impoverished, and battling discrimination to boot. In 1860, 1.25% of Americans were enslavers.

Other horrible exaggerations include referring to America's chattel slavery as the most brutal form of slavery. Chattel slavery was not unique to America. Chattel slavery was very common throughout history and the most enduring example of chattel slavery comes from Africa where it continues today. Hereditary slaves and hereditary masters have a long history in Africa. When it comes to brutality, the Arab slave trade practice of castrating males without anesthetic is quite brutal, but so is the primary reason for slaves in the Middle East and other parts of Asia. The Arab slave trade focused on women and girls. Their trade was not motivated by profits, but rather sex. Young slave girls became "the vessel of male hubris, the mats of male pleasure ground, the malleable material to be shaped to the master's will." [259]

In the 1619 riots, did anyone wonder why statues of Lincoln were torn down? Project 1619 thoroughly eviscerated Abraham Lincoln.[260] Lincoln, the president who had the guts to take on slavery, to oversee a Civil War to end slavery, and had the political skill to gain agreement among opponents that were afraid of what could happen when 4 million people that had been slaves were free. Lincoln, the president who issued the mother of all executive orders, the Emancipation Proclamation. Lincoln, the man the most prominent African American in this period, Frederick Douglas, called "the colored man's president." [261] Lincoln, who was murdered by a white supremacist after he called for blacks to have the right to vote. Lincoln was reduced to an enslaver who never really cared about black equality. Why is the new black national anthem a song written as a tribute to Lincoln? Has the nation developed schizophrenia on slavery? We are renaming streets and tearing down statues to eliminate reminders of slavery, while declaring national holidays and anthems and revising American history to revolve around slavery.

According to the National Association of Scholars President Peter Wood, Hannah-Jones saw herself "exempt from ordinary forms of accountability." The NY Times did too. Only reluctantly, the Times responded to criticism,[262] but it did so only after Hannah-Jones won a Pulitzer Prize. Ironically this prize is awarded to writers that "adhere to the highest journalistic principles." Then again, the Pulitzer Center is the organization supplying schools with the educational materials to teach Project 1619.

Over 100 documented exaggerations, falsities and outright fictions, and Project 1619 is a source of great pride for the NY Times. Executive Editor Dean Baquet said, "I believe our country, have benefited immensely from the principled, rigorous and groundbreaking

---

[xx] This "fact" would certainly not be true in 1860 when 2/3rds of legislators and Supreme Court justices had residences in states where slavery was illegal.

journalism of Nikole and the full team of writers and editors who brought us this transformative work."[263]

One would hope that transformative works are based on truth. History cannot be fiction. History should not be a fairy tale where writers cherry pick events than modify them to convince the reader of a desired position. Project 1619 blames every problem that black communities face on slavery and racism, even an obesity epidemic. Every disproportional outcome is ipso facto rooted in slavery.

The history of medical experimentation is not a topic of school curriculums, but with Project 1619 students will learn that blacks were guinea pigs, not anyone else, just blacks. They won't learn about the German vivisection of Jews or the Japanese vivisection of Chinese. They will also not learn that human medical experimentation without consent of the study participants was common and not recognized as immoral and in need of a global code of ethics until the Nuremburg Code of 1946. This code was further refined in the Declaration of Helsinki 1964, and the Belmont Report of 1978. Seems like all of this provides important context.[264]

Students will learn that opposition to any of President Obama's positions were racist and not the positions of opponents participating in a democratic tradition to arrive at the best solutions for the people. The bottom line is that children will learn that everything in America is based on a history of slavery and racism. White oppressors and black victims. The hubris of the NY Times to write "it is finally time to tell our story truthfully" is shocking, and to do it without supplying reference citations. There is a very distinct maliciousness in their words that they rationalize by calling it hard history. All nations have episodes of hard history. Many bury it. We're the only ones that exaggerate it, elevate it, and falsify it to make it worse.

Still, Project 1619 is being taught in schools all over the country, and America lives with a summer of 1619 riots. America's new "historian" of the record is not a respected historian, in fact she is not a historian at all. It is a woman that verifiably falsified history. A woman that implied that respected historians behaving decorously in their refutations of her tale, were old white racists. Like many others she knows that any conversation can be shut down, and anyone's credibility destroyed by calling or implying that they are racist.

It's hard to imagine the impact that Project 1619 will continue to have on race relations, and on the motives and ambitions of students. Children are being taught that blacks are victims of white oppression, and they are being reminded of a period when blacks were mistakenly seen as inferior. For blacks, instead of having a chance to escape a narrative of victimhood, victimhood will be reinforced. Equality of opportunity will be lost to a belief that blacks have no chance. Just as badly, reminders of historical trauma will lead to hatred towards whites.[265] White children will feel shame, so will Latino, Native American, black, and Asian children. It won't be hard for children to do their own research. Latinos will discover that they too are born with the so-called original sins of slavery and racism. In fact, they were born with it 150 years before the Americans. Their ancestors owned 19 times as many black slaves, and racism is alive and well in their homelands today. Native Americans will be torn with shame too, because they too were enslavers of blacks, and also Native Americans long before white people arrived. Latinos with Amerindian ancestors will find that their ancestors were enslavers too. Black children can feel the most shame. Their ancestors sold them into slavery. If not for their ancestors the Latinos, white Americans, and Native Americans would not have engaged in black slavery. (The Black Supremacy chapter covers this in more detail). Asian students will learn that they were once excluded as immigrants and many of their homelands have immigrant exclusions today that includes nearly everyone. Their nations really will qualify as systemically racist. Teaching this new history can easily have unintended consequences like motivating struggle sessions that existed in the Chinese Cultural Revolution. That didn't go well, and this will not either.

Already we are seeing a rise in slavery metaphors. African American NFL player Marcellus Bennett offered his assessment of race in the NFL: "The fact is the nfl, much like this country, was built on the back of black athletes. And they used the same systems that were designed during slavery and slave trade as a model to build it."[266] His brother, NFL player Michael Bennett, accused the NCAA of slavery. [267] Marcellus and Michael have annual average salaries of $7 million and $8.3 million respectively. African American Congressman from New York Jamaal Bowman said: "I believe our current system of capitalism is slavery by another name." "We've moved from physical chattel enslavement and physical racial segregation to a plantation economic system.[268] Forty-four-year-old Bowman, a former middle school principal, has a net worth that puts him in the millionaire category. African America NCAA basketball player, Geo Baker compared having to isolate from his girlfriend during the pandemic and not being able to sell his jersey, etc. as "modern day slavery."[269] He is on a full basketball scholarship and if he passes his internship in the NCAA, he can expect an average annual NBA salary of $10 million.

In 2021, African American PBS commentator Yamiche Alcindor compared the practice of separating children and parents/ "guardians" that were illegally smuggled into the United States at the southern border with separating parents and children during the Middle Passage in the Atlantic slave trade.[xxi,270,271] To stay with the comparison to slavery, her MSNBC host could have asked Alcindor about the separation of black parents and children today. There are "more black children today that grow up without their two biological parents than there was during slavery."[272]

Project 1776. Project 1776 has gotten far less attention than Project 1619. It is sponsored by the Woodson Center. It is an endeavor of a diverse group of intellectuals and activists. African American Bob Woodson leads the Center. Glenn Loury said encouraging black victimhood is very unhelpful because victims are subordinates, and subordinates are by definition inferior. [273] Woodson agrees. "We are building a positive movement in response to the overwhelming narratives of oppression, grievance and ignorance to America's history — and its promise for the future." [274] The Woodson Center celebrates the mettle of black people that have not only survived a history of slavery but have demonstrated extraordinary achievement and are a source of inspiration for all immigrants and all people. "The future of black America is not defined by slavery." We don't subscribe to a "race grievance industry." [275] Unfortunately, the narrative of black victims is preferred to black greatness past, present, and in the future. Race hustlers and poverty pimps find the sordid tale of Project 1619 much more useful.

[xxi] Separating children from their parent(s) at the border has been done for nearly two decades for various reasons like, human smugglers provide discounts for adults with children, even if they are not their own because it is simpler for them to enter the United States and be granted asylum. The Health and Human Service commission keeps close tabs on separate children and children have many legal protections.

Project 1945. Project 1945 is a proposed endeavor of the Kathleen Brush Foundation. This project covers a chapter in American history that schools do not teach. All nations have histories of slavery, but only America has a history of unparalleled influence ending discrimination in the world. The choice of 1945 is because there is no year more important to the history of discrimination. Prior to 1945, nations didn't see discrimination; they saw ordered societies. That changed in 1945 when President Franklin Delano Roosevelt parlayed American victory in WWII to convince global powers to end the colonial subjugation of Africans, Asians, and Europeans all over the world, and to get all nations to commit to ending discrimination. In 1945, the death knell was sounding for white supremacy in the world. In 1964, America was the first nation to pronounce it dead. By the early 1970s, America had created the first anti-racist *system* of governance. Outside the white-majority western nations, most other nations ignored their commitments, and discrimination continued as it had before 1945. That's why in the 21st century you can still find select, but often very large, groups experiencing slavery, arbitrary imprisonment, stateless populations and garden variety legally sanctioned privileged and unprivileged populations common in systemically racist systems. Discrimination continued as it always had.

Children being taught truthfully about America's leading roles in: (1) ending colonial subordination all over the world; (2) encouraging all nations to deliver equal fundamental freedoms to all regardless of their "race, colour, sex, language, religion, political or other opinion, national or social origin, property, birth or other status;" [276] and (3) creating a world beating anti-racist system to reverse a racist past is a very important chapter in American history.

The voices of social justice have no interest in presenting an accurate portrayal of America as the first woke nation, the first global advocate of social justice and the world's anti-racist leader. There is a much greater appetite to applaud people that falsely alter and denigrate American history and cast many great Americans as despicable people. Instead of a nation of great honor, our nation is cast as a nation of great horrors.[277] The nation and the accomplishments of our ancestors are being sacrificed because there must be a way to explain the disproportional lack of progress for blacks relative to other people of color. [278]

Project 1619 crafts a story to rationalize the underperformance of blacks. It goes like this; it is due to white oppression that was first embedded in slavery and continued on in the form of racism. It's a perfect story for why blacks fare disproportionately poorly relative to Asian-, Latino-, Nigerian-, and Jewish Americans. It's a story obliterated by global and American history, but in the world of CRT, stories can omit and exaggerate what they like. Just like the whopper told by Project 1619. Blacks permanently victimized by an old and dated history of white oppression. Loury said: "the first axiom to the credo of racial loyalty is that when blacks fail, it is whites who are responsible."[279]

Nothing is more powerful than the race card. In this case, the power will carry many negative outcomes for blacks, whites and all Americans. The only ones gaining from the perpetuation of victimhood through an exaggerated and falsified history of American slavery are poverty pimps and race hustlers.

Black Supremacy Preceded White Supremacy

Reports regularly surface of college students that don't know who won the civil war, or who America fought in the Revolutionary War. Adults, in general fair no better. One study found 50% of Americans didn't know what the three branches of government were. Another study showed that eighty-two percent of 8th graders were found not proficient in US history.[280] These are the results in a nation where most schools are required to teach American history. About a quarter of states, require a course in world history. One study called the knowledge that US students have of other nations as "weak and increasingly dangerous." [281] It makes sense that Americans fair so poorly on the topic of American history; surveys regularly show that Americans find history uninteresting. It also makes sense that school administrators don't find world history important enough to qualify for inclusion in school curriculums. If students find American history boring, the history of the world would surely put them to sleep.

It is curious that Americans have become obsessed with the history of slavery in America. The combined obsession and deficit of historical knowledge offers a plausible answer for why Project 1619 could falsely rewrite history and it would be rapidly adopted. Or why White Fragility author Robin Diangelo could build on a notion also raised in Roots and the Amistad that white people roamed Africa lassoing blacks and enslaving them, seemingly without pushback. It also makes sense that it took professional historians to see that Project 1619 was propaganda. The severe "dangerous" deficiency of American knowledge of other nations would further explain why best-selling author Ibram Kendi could call African chiefs selling their people an anachronistic memory.[282] Face it. Americans are easily fooled when writers recreate the history of America or the world.

Let's have a look at some unadulterated history of slavery in America with an Afrocentric approach. This means learning about slavery in Africa.[283]

Westerners are quite unusual in being forthright with parts of history, like slavery, that others are diligent about burying. The context of slavery in the United States starts with Portugal creating colonies in west Africa in the 15th century. It was evident to the Portuguese that chattel slavery was quite normal in Africa, and African traders were interested in new buyers and markets. It's possible that there never would have been an Atlantic slave trade and the Americas would be overwhelmingly white, just like Europe, if these discoveries were never made. But the discoveries were made, and the Atlantic slave trade did exist. For 458 years, Portugal and Spain counted among the grandest buyers for slaves in Africa that would travel across the Atlantic. Almost all were sold to Spanish and Portuguese settlers in Latin America. Several nations in Latam were called slave economies, because more people were slaves than free. The trading in slaves in the Thirteen Colonies only came in the mid to latter part of the 17th century. But why would Europe's early settlers in America even think about slavery. Northern Europe had made slavery part of its history long before the 17th century, and it had ended chattel slavery before that. Settlers in the Thirteen Colonies did need extra labor and for 50-60 years they leveraged indentured servants that were black but mostly white.

Later in the 17th century the Thirteen Colonies began buying slaves. Why did Americans switch from indentured servitude for blacks and whites, to servitude for whites and chattel slavery for blacks? This was a time when it was illegal to enslave Christians, and it was a time when colonists learned that chattel slavery was part of African culture.

By the time the United States abolished the purchase of slaves in the early 1800s, she had acquired 388,000 slaves from the Atlantic trade. When the purchase of slaves ended in Latam in the late 1800s more the 10 million had been bought.

How did some white folks manage to acquire enslaved Africans that came from the middle of Africa? Answering this requires knowledge of the internal African slave trades, the Arab slave trade, and the involvement of Africans in the trade. Getting the content for this context is not straightforward. "Most of the African authors have not yet published a book on the Arab-Muslim slave trade out of religious solidarity. There are 500 million Muslims in Africa, and it is better to blame the West than talk about the past crimes of Arab Muslims." [284] Like the castration of 17 million African men and the murder of an unknown number of mulatto infants.[285] African authors have also chosen to downplay African involvement, which was critical to the trade for the same reason. Better to blame remorseful white westerners who have generously documented their involvement. All this notwithstanding, a proper accounting of history shows that there is plenty of blame to go around. Within all this blame one conclusion seems obvious. Without slavery being normal in Africa and without African traders, indeed entire African "nations" willing to meet foreign demands, white supremacy over blacks in America would never have occurred because black populations in the Americas would have been virtually non-existent. White supremacy over blacks in the United States required black-on-black supremacy in Africa. It is in Africa that the so-called original sin of black slavery was committed. If there is a special original sin for whites enslaving blacks it was born in the Middle East in the 7th century.

Sustaining the demand for slaves in Africa, western and south Asia, and the Americas required an African feeder system that employed many thousands of Africans. Fueling the Arab trade was especially demanding because an estimated 70-80% died, many during a rudimentary castration process.[286] Entire African villages and tribes relied on selling Africans. Friends and family sold friends and family, and ordinary people engaged in kidnapping soon-to-be slaves. According to Koelle's informants, 40% of slaves were kidnapped or seized by Africans, 24% were war captives, 19% tricked by a friend or relative, and 19% enslaved by judicial sentences.[287]

> "Our people traded extensively in slaves. It was a dangerous trade, but very profitable. It was dangerous, because you must be strong enough to overpower your victim. Secondly, you must be prepared to risk your life, wresting children from their parents, and so on."
> Nkwonto Nwuduaku in Urunnebo, October 16, 1974[288]

> "The successful sale of adults was considered an exploit for which a man was hailed by praise singers, akin to exploits in wrestling, war, or in hunting animals like the lion." This was still so in the 20th century.[289]

African slave traders saw an unusually rich economic opportunity in the Americas. Arab slave traders preferred women and girls. In Africa the demand was primarily for women and children. Male slaves were commonly killed because they caused too much trouble. Now they formed a lucrative opportunity in the Americas. [290] About 65% of slaves to the Americas were men.

When the British tried to end slavery in 19th century colonial Africa, they were rebuffed by Africans who found these white supremacists ignorant of African culture. Africans continued selling slaves in Africa and Asia, but the end of the Atlantic trade led to a glut. "Those [African] families which were really rich competed with one another in the number of slaves each killed for its dead or used to placate the gods." [291]

The land for Liberia in Africa was purchased by the American Colonization Society in 1822. Liberia was to be a new home for free blacks from America because it was felt that blacks could not escape discrimination or a history of slavery in the United States. There is irony that whites too would be unable to escape a history of slavery. Americo-Liberians created a constitution in 1847 that prohibited slavery. But slavery was normal in Africa. Americo-Liberians found constitutional work arounds that leveraged traditional methods of enslavement like pawning children or wives. In 1962 slavery officially ended in Liberia, but it may have persisted without the strong encouragement to end it from white westerners in the League of Nations and later the United Nations. [292] Liberia was not the last African nation to agree to abolish slavery. That was Mauritania in 1981, but an estimated 10-20% of people are still slaves. Agreeing to abolish slavery is often an agreement to create a law; enforcement is optional. Today, Arab and African slave traders still ply their trade in Mauritania and the Sudan, and slavery persists in many parts of Africa.

About 15% of America's slaves were people born as slaves from the Igbo tribe in today's Nigeria. In 2018, the practice of designating Nigerian Igbo people as slaves at birth was abolished, but some African relatives of Americans still struggle to merge and marry freeborn people. Are the enslavers remorseful? No. Do the once enslaved demand recompense? It is an absurd notion to seek an apology for something that permeates African history and was culturally ingrained. Enslavers were admired. What these former slaves want is to be treated like ordinary freeborn people. Then, perhaps, they can have a chance for a better life.

It's hard to imagine the different views that Africans had toward slavery and human life. Slavery and slave trading legally existed in Africa for more than a millennium before the Atlantic slave trade began and more than 200 years after. It's challenging to think about African merchants being hailed for hunting people in the same vein as lions into the 20th century. It is also hard to fathom that there would have been no black slavery in the United States, if blacks enslaving blacks in Africa was not culturally ordinary.

In today's environment there is an absurd notion that only white people dominated people from other races/ethnicities. Equally absurd, white supremacy is portrayed as a permanent condition predicated on a culturally ingrained desire to subordinate blacks. This would make it incomprehensible to acknowledge that it is western values, power and influence in the 19th and 20th centuries that drove the abolition of slavery across the world. Without these western efforts, black slavery might still be widespread in Africa and the Middle East, rather than limited. For the westerners, it was not an easy sell, because the view of slavery as immoral was not widely shared, and prohibitions on slavery were often dismissed as westerners imposing their views on others.

To gain a proper context for slavery in the United States one has to combine Eurocentric and Afrocentric history as told by erudite scholars of history, not editors, journalists, and social justice philanthropists smitten with having the power to rewrite history with the stroke of a pen and the chance to make America a scapegoat for strife in black communities. [293]

An Obsession with Discrimination and More Snake Oil

Anytime academic rigor is deprioritized, and storytelling is prioritized, there should be an expectation of some real whoppers. This is a big problem because the whoppers are being accepted. The "theory" of intersectionality was born in the mind of a black female lawyer and CRT advocate that seems obsessed with discrimination against black women. The "theory" of white privilege was born in the mind of an apparently guilt-ridden white woman in the late 1980s wondering about the many ways that whites had privilege. White fragility was born in the eccentric mind of another ostensibly guilt-ridden white woman. A formula for being an anti-racist that requires racism as an antidote was born in the mind of a male black professor that writes while oozing hatred for whites. The Melanin Theory was born in the mind of a black anti-Semitic professor seeking a theory for black superiority to counter the falsified belief in biological determinism.

Theory of Intersectionality. Both the "theory" of intersectionality, which is a CRT offshoot, and CRT are alike in one very salient view. Both assume that Americans, and most saliently white Americans, are obsessed with discrimination against blacks.

African American lawyer Kimberlé Crenshaw drove interest in the subject of intersecting stereotypes when she introduced the "theory" of intersectionality in 1989. Her "theory" tries to explain how people with multiple characteristics that can drive isms, like racism and sexism, will experience discrimination that is different from just being, for example, black or a woman because the isms are interconnected. People possessing multiple isms must therefore be treated by the courts as unique entities to accurately assess if they have faced discrimination. Her theory is not specific to any intersecting biases, but of particular interest to Crenshaw was the intersection of being black and a woman. She saw a judge could dismiss a discrimination claim by a black woman, because an employer did not discriminate against blacks or women, when the blacks were men, and the women were white. Crenshaw advanced that the stereotype for black plus the stereotype for women did not equal the stereotype for black women and could not explain the specific biases that black women face. This made the logic of a judge that took this path flawed. Was the logic flawed? In one case, the judge noted that "the prospect of the creation of new classes of protected minorities, governed only by the mathematical principles of permutation and combination, clearly raises the prospect of opening the hackneyed Pandora's box." [294]

The judge was presiding over a case evaluating alleged discrimination against women that were black, but he had to consider the precedent of permitting combinations of protected categories of people. It was an important consideration. Latino subgroups, for example, include Amerindian Latinas, Amerindian Latinos, Asian Latinas, Asian Latinos, black Latinas, black Latinos, white Latinas, white Latinos, mulatto Latinas, mulatto Latinos, mestizo Latinas, mestizo Latinos, zambo Latinas, and zambo Latinos. Now take each of these categories and add different national origins for each Latin American country. Then for each add, over age 40, bisexual, lesbian, gay, transexual, Jewish, Muslim, Catholic, Protestant…. A similar categorization process would then need to be created for black Obsessions, Asian Americans, white Americans, and Native Americans.

African American UCLA law professor, Devon Carbado and Mitu Gulati expanded intersectionality further. In their book called Acting White, they argued that there was a need to create separate legally protected classes for combinations that went beyond unchangeable physical aspects and included appearances and behaviors. For example, in the case of black women, a woman could face discrimination because she was acting white or acting black, or even looking white, for example with straight hair or looking black, with dreadlocks. CRT based, the supportive data to validate the expansion of the "theory" of intersectionality is built on hypothetical stories. [295]

The courts could not deal with intersectionality based on combinations from Title VII protected classes, let alone appearances and behaviors. The combinations and permutations would be overwhelming. Another huge problem is that the definition of intersectionality is a subject of great debate that continually mutates. One could imagine that developing a legal definition(s) of intersectionality would surely inspire wrath from people with complex identities and behaviors that saw the law as deficient.

The theory of intersectionality has never been evaluated beyond some anecdotes. Remember it's based on CRT – stories not data. Still, its predictive ability would falter, because stereotypes are very fallible as predictors of discriminatory acts. Besides, even a cursory review of available research shows the theory to be problematic. This includes research that has found people that fall into multiple protected categories, as all people do, may not cause people to create new stereotypes that yield different biases, because people that have unconsciously biased thoughts, have a tendency to focus on one instigator of bias. For example, in the case of a black woman, if woman is chosen, black biases are submerged and vice versa.[296] This seems to make some sense. A person, for example, might have developed or learned a stereotype for Asian people or lesbians, but not for Asian lesbians let alone an over 40 Asian lesbian that is Vietnamese, 4'11 and overweight. Indeed, the presence of multiple characteristics that could drive biases could lead to less or no discrimination because people become "metaphorically invisible."[297] These positions contrast with what seems like an assumption that people are obsessed with discriminating.

Being much more like a hunch than a theory doesn't preclude advocates from pretending the theory of intersectionality is useful for predicting discriminatory behaviors. For example, Crenshaw asserted that because affirmative action does not give specific accommodations to black women, it favors white women, and they are the primary beneficiaries. [298] Crenshaw's assertion has been used as a citation for others to claim white women are the primary beneficiaries of affirmative action. Now, it's become a general truth and one readily accepted because it's consistent with black victimology, and also consistent with a belief that white people unconsciously make decisions based on skin color. It is not, however consistent with the outcomes of affirmative actions.

One study found that "affirmative action has no significant influence on their [white women] employment, even at higher job levels."[299] Crenshaw's assertion that white women are the primary beneficiaries may have been influenced by white women being the largest population on college campuses, but this is because white women are the largest group to apply for college, and also meet admission requirements for GPA and SAT/ACT scores. It has nothing to do with affirmative action. Affirmative action, and like policies, work against white women. At elite institutions, like Dartmouth, "the demographic that gets squeezed is the white middle class." [300] Because women are now a majority on college campuses, white women get squeezed even more because colleges strive for gender parity too.[301] Still, Crenshaw's assertion pervades discussions about the need to eliminate white women, and not just from affirmative action programs but also from diversity targets.

Deconstructing White Privilege. Most people don't know that white privilege, like CRT and the theory of intersectionality originated in 1989. In the past three decades, progress diminishing discrimination in America has been so rapid, thirty-two years might as well be 100 years.

The inventor of white privilege was a white woman named Peggy McIntosh. She reasoned that being a member of the majority race offered "an invisible package of unearned privileges." She then conjured up a list of white privileges.

The term white privilege has caught on like wildfire. It's become a catch phrase to rationalize any situation where whites have fared well compared to blacks, Latinos, and Native Americans. (Asians were initially included in these comparisons, but for obvious reasons they are not any longer.) Most whites have worked really hard to get where they are, and they are offended when they are told they have white privilege. They don't see privilege, but they don't know what white privilege means, and nor do 99.99% of the people that use the term. McIntosh provides a checklist of twenty items that define white privileges. Below are eleven from the list.

1. "My culture gives me little fear about ignoring the perspectives and powers of people of other races."
2. "I can worry about racism without being seen as self-interested or self-seeking."
3. "I can be pretty sure that an argument with a colleague of another race is more likely to jeopardize her/his chances for advancement than to jeopardize mine."
4. "I can be pretty sure of having my voice heard in a group in which I am the only member of my race."
5. "I can turn on the television or open the front page of the paper and see people of my race widely represented."
6. "I can go into a music shop and count on finding music of my race represented."
7. "I can choose blemish cover or bandages in "flesh color" and have them more or less match the color of my skin."
8. "I can be sure that my children will be given curricular materials that testify to the existence of their race."
9. "I can easily find academic courses and institutions which give attention only to people of my race."
10. "I can be pretty sure that if I ask to talk with the person in charge, I will be facing a person of my race."
11. "I can talk with my mouth full and not have people put this down to my color." [302]

Confused? You might even think that this could be in part a black privilege checklist, in part, a who cares checklist, and in part a very dated checklist.

White privilege is derived from the notion that a race/ethnicity, or in some cases a religion in the majority have benefits that makes life more comfortable, a comfort that smaller populations do not have. American whites are hardly the only majority population. Virtually every county has a majority race/ethnicity, or religion, and the majority race/ethnicity or religion has privilege. For example, there are forty-five countries that have Sunni-Muslim-privilege. Three countries have Shia-Muslim privilege. In China there is Han Chinese privilege. In Russia, ethnic Russian privilege. In Japan, Japanese privilege. In South Africa, black privilege. Keep in mind; these aren't perfect analogies because none of the just noted nations have endeavored to create multiracial societies, and so people in the majority might have privileges that are quantifiably more valuable than flesh tone band-aids, and they really might not feature minorities on television, in the music industry, or include them in history, and most would not give minorities a voice of any substance. Quite realistically, they might repress narratives of minority victimization and majority oppression as self-interested and self-seeking. Further, none would be promoting immigration policies to forego their majority. In the United States, the estimated white population in 1700 was 95%, in 1863 87%, 1989 76%, and 2020 60% non-Hispanic white. In more than half of all American cities and six states, there is no white majority. California and Texas, the two most populated states, have minority majorities. White privilege RIP.

The Melanin Theory, Free Speech on College Campuses and Anti-Semitism. The Melanin Theory was an invention of African American Professor Leonard Jeffries. The "theory" proposes that blacks have greater intelligence and spiritual qualities because of the melanin in their skin. They are also warmer and more humanistic compared to cold and materialistic whites. Whites have a dog-eat-dog mentality while blacks are cooperative. Jeffries maintains that his theory cannot be falsified using "Eurocentric methods," which generally makes it impossible for whites to scientifically refute. While the Melanin "theory" sounds like a racist theory, Jeffries claims his theory is not racist because he is simply explaining racial difference. Thirty years later, Ibram Kendi from Boston University asserts something similar. When he calls all whites racist, the word "racist is not a pejorative…It is descriptive." [303] Chinese social networkers have a similar take for expressing beliefs that blacks are ignorant criminals. They aren't racist because they are true descriptions.[304]

What of Jeffries views about Jews? Were these racist? In 1991, he made a speech where he said Jews financed the slave trade, controlled Hollywood, and ran his employer, the City College of New York. He made a specific reference to the head Jew at the college. The college terminated him, but he was reinstated and paid $400,000 in damages (about $800,000 today) because his termination was based on freedom of speech. The college went on to apologize for discouraging him from "speaking his mind." [305] It's hard to believe this took place so recently. Today, many college campuses can't advocate for free speech, because they fear the consequences. Instead, they practice censorship. The people with views that are most likely to face discrimination and be censored are people with conservative views that factually argue against blacks being victims of oppressive whites, or that argue America is not a racist society, and cops are not a roving band of white supremacists. These views are seen as disrespectful, insensitive, hate speech, and of course racist.[306,307] Meanwhile in 2020, students at the University of Illinois and Colombia University passed a resolution calling for divestment from any organizations that support Israel. The president of Colombia disagreed with the resolution and had no intentions of discriminating against Jews, but any word about student racists or censoring these views was missing. [308] On colleges, it's okay to protect free speech for people that are racist against Jews, but not for people that are racist against whites, or falsely present America or cops as racist.

Jeffries had many disciples. One was Kristen Clarke, an Assistant Secretary of Civil Rights under President Biden.[xxii] As a student of Harvard, she advanced the Melanin "theory" as a counterargument to the Bell Curve and called on Bell Curve authors Murray and Herrnstein to refute the Melanin Theory. Harvard responded by saying that "serious researchers of the issue no more have to take into account the melanin theory than those searching for extraterrestrial life have to take into account every UFO nut who claims to have been abducted." [309] Good for Harvard in the 1990s. Would they take that position today, or would they cower from a possible accusation of racism?

Like Jeffries, Clarke has also supported anti-Semitism. Clarke says she has moved on and she is now committed to fighting anti-Semitism. She is also committed to fighting white supremacy. Since the latter died in 1964, seems like a focus on anti-Semitism might be more deserving, and focusing on black anti-Semitism would seem like the best use of time. Blacks are nearly 2.3 times as likely as whites to be anti-Semitic. [xxiii, xxiv, 310]

Anti-racist formulas that call for more racism and infantilizing blacks. There are two best-selling CRT storytellers that offer big ideas for addressing perceptions of discrimination in America by advancing bizarre anti-racist formulas. One calls for more racism and the other for infantilizing blacks.

Ibram Kendi, author of How to Be an Antiracist is a storyteller of the first order. His book reads like an anti-white polemic, but he has said he doesn't hate white people. "How can you hate a group of people for who they are?" [311] Louis Farrakhan said something similar in 2000: "White people are potential humans - they haven't evolved yet." Kendi, like Reverend Jeremiah Wright, also accused whites of creating AIDS to commit genocide on blacks. Like Wright, Farrakhan, and Sharpton[xxv] he has also been on the wrong side of anti-Semitism or the people that promote it. Very different from Wright and Farrakhan, is the respect afforded Kendi by people like those at the Bill & Melinda Gates Foundation.

In Kendi's rambling first-person story/memoir/propaganda piece, he has re-popularized an old, tired message that you are either a racist or an anti-racist. You cannot be a person that is color blind or that treats all people equally. This is the same as being a racist. Got that all you folks that have prided yourself on being egalitarian – you are racists. If you are not spending your days thinking about the narrative of black victimhood and how you as an oppressor can deliver equity, you are a racist.

You might think a college professor would deal with facts, but as a CRT acolyte, stories are weighted over facts. When he dabbles with facts, like the writers of Project 1619, he gets tangled up in the truth. For Kendi's story to work, he needs for America to be the inventor of slavery based on race. He deprioritizes nearly 200 years of slavery in Latin America that occurred prior to slavery in the United States and draws a sharp contrast with the Arab slave trade. He casts this trade as not racist because the Arab traders enslaved blacks, whites and Asians. Because it's not racist, it is anti-racist. And anti-racism is good,

---

[xxii] Clarke was not confirmed on 2/24/21.

[xxiii] Foreign born Latinos are 3 times as likely as whites. US born Latinos are 1.9 times as likely.

[xxiv] "The most well-educated Americans are remarkably free of prejudicial views, while less educated Americans are more likely to hold anti-Semitic views." Anti-Defamation League.

[xxv] Sharpton is held responsible for riots against Jews in 1991 in the Crown Heights neighborhood of Brooklyn following the accidental death of a black Guyanese child. Sharpton called Jews, diamond merchants who profited from South African apartheid, then ran down black kids on the street.

right? It's hard to see the extremely cruel slavery that was based on religion as good. [312] It's also hard to reconcile how a "leading anti-racist" can think slavery based on anything is good, unless he relishes the misery of non-blacks. Seeing the Arab slave trade as anti-racist and less bad, is something supported by Project 1619 which saw slavery in America as more brutal and "unlike anything that had existed in the world before." Both Kendi and 1619 have made an incredibly ignorant assertion. The Arabs enslaved far more blacks than were enslaved in the Atlantic trade. There are few traces of blacks in the Middle East today because these traders did what they could to prevent black slaves from ever having descendants. Seventy to eighty percent of slaves in this trade perished. Two common causes of death were castration and infanticide. [313] Seems pretty racist, no?

To Kendi, African involvement in the slave trade is a sideshow. "The idea that "African chiefs" sold their "own people" is an anachronistic memory." [314] Slavery and slave trading in 21st century Africa doesn't seem to do justice to the anachronistic descriptor. The horrors of 1300 years of Arabs and Africans working together to run a trade in black humans hardly seems like a black slavery sideshow. But for Kendi's narrative of Americans inventing slavery based on race and an irredeemably racist America, a racism he describes as metastatic, like metastatic cancer, African involvement must be whitewashed from history.

Kendi shares something else in common with Project 1619. He is helping to promote CRT in schools. His anti-white polemic has become part of the Fairfax County, Virginia school curriculum. Before adopting his book, Kendi was paid $20,000 to share with his audience that "the only remedy to past discrimination is present discrimination." His anti-racist formula calls for blacks discriminating against whites. It's an equity thing. It's an idea stolen from an extremist and Marxist group called the Black Panthers. They called for fighting racism with racism, rationalizing their racism as justified. Implementing Kendi's anti-racist formula, like the Black Panthers' formula, is unconstitutional. [315,316] Hence, the need for the constitutional amendment Kendi proposed to permit discrimination that facilitates equity. As you might imagine if you don't support the amendment you are a racist.

A black scholar on racism, said Kendi is "ultimately teaching the reader less about how to be antiracist than about how to be anti-intellectual." [317] Kendi seems like a very odd choice on many levels for advising Fairfax County schools on anti-racism and as the author of teaching materials for their students. Kendi is further a very odd choice for leading the Anti-Racist Research Institute at American University in Washington D.C. How can a racist be an anti-racist leader?

Professor Robin DiAngelo, the best-selling author of White Fragility, is another acolyte of CRT that cements blacks as victims of white oppression. She is also another storyteller extraordinaire. Her primary message is that "all white people are invested in and collude with racism." A key part of her story relies on whites as born racists. "Racism is a social system embedded in the culture and its institutions. We are born into this system and have no say in whether we will be affected by it." [318]

Like Kendi, DiAngelo's "theory" relies on bastardizing history. She casts Americans as genocidaires of Native Americans that also stole their land. The 1619 Project takes this latter position too. This is an important claim to cement this forever story of racist America. It is true that Native Americans as well as the indigenous populations in Latin America and Australia were devastated by the diseases of white men for which they had no natural defenses. Genocide, however, requires a deliberate intent to wipe out a population. What happened to Native Americans, and Amerindians and Aborigines was not genocide. That is what happened to the Jews in WWII and the Tutsis in Rwanda in 1994. Land theft is also a fiction.[319,320] But these stories must be accepted, for her story to hold. And it has held. White Fragility was a NY Times best seller for over two years. The secret to her success, just like other poverty pimps and race hustlers is she exploits knowing that white people are terrorized at the thought of being racists. But she gives white people an out. They can't help themselves because it's in the system. She is another writer alluding to the inability to dispense with the original sin of slavery.[321]

African American Professor John McWhorter commenting on DiAngelo's book said: "In 2020—as opposed to 1920—I neither need nor want anyone to muse on how whiteness privileges them over me. Nor do I need wider society to undergo teachings in how to be exquisitely sensitive about my feelings… I cannot imagine that any Black readers could willingly submit themselves to DiAngelo's ideas while considering themselves adults of ordinary self-regard and strength. Few books about race have more openly infantilized Black people than this supposedly authoritative tome."[322]

Another leading African American thinker on race relations, Coleman Hughes, said of DiAngelo's book "this is where the book borders on actual racism — is that black people are emotionally immature and essentially child-like. Blacks, as portrayed in DiAngelo's writing, can neither be expected to show maturity during disagreement nor to exercise emotional self-control of any kind. The hidden premise of the book is that blacks, not whites, are too fragile." [323]

How has DiAngelo managed to sell to white people that talking down to black people will help to assuage the guilt of being born racists? Do white people feel better when they see blacks as incapable? If black people are offended by her anti-racist formula and see it as racist, why do white people think it's an antidote to the guilt of having unconsciously raised their guard when walking down a dark street and encountering an unfamiliar black man.

Consider a situation in the NFL. The NFL's initial response to football players kneeling during the national anthem was pointed to as proof of white fragility. The NFL later decided to disregard fan abandonment, [xxvi] address their fragility and embrace that blacks are victims of white oppression. Paternalism is a natural response to address fragility and victims. Here is how one of the leading NFL social justice advocates, Marcellus Bennett, responded: "All these coaches with white daddy syndrome in the league and football period talking down to black players in a way they would never do to a white player know it's wrong then want to turn around and tell em im hard on because I love you like you're my own son as an excuse."[324] Well, that didn't go well. Paternalism was seen as racist, just like Hughes noted above, but so was supporting respect for the National Anthem. What a quandary. Any position white's take is racist.

The current painting of white Americans as born racists has not been helpful.[325] Being falsely accused of being a racist is a venomous accusation. It's analogous to the worst of racial slurs. Being called a racist is not as Kendi says, just a descriptor. That's the position of a race hustler, and he's laughing all the way to the bank.

[xxvi] 2016 was the first-year players started kneeling for the national anthem. Viewership dropped 8% that year. In 2020 the kneeling was revived along with the black national anthem. Viewership is down 10%.

So many are in on the con. Bastardize history, leverage a quack theory, create new quack theories, take advantage of white guilt, reinforce the narrative of black victimhood, and take comfort that opposing positions will be marginalized. They are all tricks of the trade from a growing population of poverty pimps and race hustlers.

The Oxymoronic Racist Rule of Law

It would be impossible to have a nation rich with protected freedoms, like the United States, without rule of law. This is why America has always had a steadfast commitment to rule of law. If people disrespected the law, "the streets in your community would quickly become a chaotic and less safe place. Police officers might be overwhelmed trying to help the situation or ignored altogether."[326]

Social justice. Rule of law is, however, being compromised. Equality before the law is seen as discriminatory because some crimes are *committed* by some races/ethnicities disproportionately to their population. Rather than looking at why this occurs, for example, disproportionate educational outcomes and a breakdown of the two-parent family, and trying to fix that, the simpler solution for politicians, although not law-abiding citizens, is to wrongly impugn the criminal justice system as systemically racist and pass "equity-oriented" laws. Ignoring the reality of political expediency and pandering to social justice constituents, this makes cosmic negative sense, but that isn't stopping the creation of two criminal justice systems. One administers justice per the rule of law and the other social justice. In the latter case, the personal morals of individual politicians and judges take precedence over law. Scofflaws are given social justice, and rule abiding citizens can find no justice at all. The outcome won't be good. When right and wrong become ambiguous and are unevenly applied, there is chaos. The safety of people and property and the foundation of American democracy is jeopardized.

How can judges use personal morals to decide justice? The arbitrary administration of justice violates the oath of office taken by every judge: "I, Judge So and So, do solemnly swear (or affirm) that I will administer justice without respect to persons, and do equal right to the poor and to the rich, and that I will faithfully and impartially discharge and perform all the duties incumbent upon me as some judge under the Constitution and laws of the United States. So help me God." With social justice, adhering to oaths, like laws, appears to be optional.

Social justice in action. Beginning in 2019/2020 some cities began formally or informally halting the prosecution of what are called survival crimes. Behind this is the notion that people in poverty engage in crimes for survival. Seattle, Washington is staking out a position of leadership in the "poverty defense." Momentum for this first surfaced during the regular protests and riots by BLM activists in 2020, with continuation into 2021.[xxvii,327]

The idea behind survival crimes is that in order to survive or whatever, people might, for example, steal food, perhaps dine and dash, pitch a tent on private property, sell drugs, engage in prostitution or assault someone to get money for food or something else *they need*. Instead of relying on law, perpetrators are to be judged based on personal stories. If their stories entail drug addiction, mental impairment, or low-income that should constitute a successful poverty defense. Even before legislation has been passed, some Seattle stores have closed up shop because they can't absorb the theft from *people in need*. This is a situation of social justice for the law breakers and no justice of any kind for hardworking people. The privileged people?

One of the black leaders Seattle has relied on to craft a dual system of social justice and no justice, is former pimp, Andre Taylor. Street czar is Andre's title. A richly rewarded

---

[xxvii] Blacks are 7% of the population, but 17% of the impoverished.

profession paying $150,000 year. Taylor said a "street czar is a person who has a particular genius in a particular area… Black people as a whole have not been in a place to be compensated for their genius or their work for a very very long time." [328] He must have missed the millions that have flowed into the coffers of Jesse Jackson and Al Sharpton. Sharpton, who visited the White House seventy times during the Obama presidency was also seen as a street genius. A White House official said of Sharpton, "He's got credibility in the community that nobody else has got. There's really no one else out there who does what he does."[329] It's true. There aren't a lot of people that are motivated to instigate racism against whites and demotivate the people they are supposed to be leading by telling them that they aren't responsible for any troubles they have because they are victims of white oppression.

Seattle's street czar was asked to help vacate BLM activists from the CHOP/CHAZ area of downtown Seattle in 2020. This was during what Seattle's white leftist Mayor Jenny Durkan called the Summer of Love. Taylor advised the activists not to leave without getting paid to leave. He told them he thought he could get them $2 million.[330] Hustler Taylor overestimated how guilty the city leaders were feeling about the victims of a love zone where 6 were shot, 3 fatally. In an autonomous zone, where Carmen Best, the African American police chief said, the police were unable to respond to "rapes, robberies, and all sorts of violent acts." [331]

In 2014, Seattle became the first city in the nation to pass an ordinance requiring a $15 minimum wage. Since this time, Seattle's property crime rate has been rising and is now double the rate in Washington state. [332] Increases in property crime are a known problem with increases in the minimum wage. The National Bureau of Economic Research tied escalations in property crime to increases in minimum wages. The greater the increase the more the crime. This is never suggested in the promotional messages supporting the increases. It's more likely voters would see a message like raising the minimum wage prevents tens of thousands of crimes as fewer people are "forced to turn to illegal activity to make ends meet." [333] Who turns to property crime? Young people with fewer skills and lower educational attainment that cannot find jobs at the higher wages. Young blacks and Latinos are the most affected.

Seattle police no longer investigate unattended property crimes. People that have been robbed are advised to contact their insurance companies. This virtual legality is another reason property crime has been rising. The legal system encourages it. This is another form of social justice for criminals and no justice for the victims of crime. The police have also been told to turn a blind eye to crimes committed by the homeless. The goal is to eliminate "racial disproportionality." Blacks and Native Americans are disproportionately homeless in Seattle. [334] The case is being made that rule of law must be sacrificed for equity for the homeless.[335]

Seattle is the 18th largest city and has less crime than 4% of US cities. Most crime is property crime, and it is disproportionately committed by blacks. Blacks are 7% of the population, but they committed nearly a third of all crimes, and over 50% of homicides. New equity measures have been lowering the number of blacks and Native Americans charged with a crime, but there has been an increase for whites and Asians. That's equity. [336,337]

Seattle knew that virtually legalizing property crime would lead to increases and not just because its intuitive. As a way to reduce incarcerations, in 2014, California passed a new law that virtually legalized property theft under $950. It did reduce incarcerations, however, the increase in property crimes is sobering. Vehicle break-ins have leapt 20% to 30% in different cities. Thieves keep their hauls under $950, although the net loss to car owners is far greater due to broken windows and jimmied doors and trunks. Shoplifting has also been on a tear, and this includes organized retail theft. The thieves again keep their hauls below $950 per outing per store. Over time politicians have cheered the law for the improbable outcome of reducing crime. They know that what has occurred is people don't waste their time filling out crime reports when nothing will be done. In total, this is another social justice victory for felony burglars and a defeat for justice for the victims of what are now non-crimes.[338,339]

In Seattle there is more to come for criminal justice reform all under the rubric of "dismantling systems of racism, oppression, and poverty." [340] Ironically, Seattle has one of the lowest rates of poverty and the highest rates of tolerance in the United States. Excepting political tolerance. King County, where Seattle resides counts among the top 2% least politically tolerant communities in the United States. Conservative views are not welcome here.[341]

Portland is another Pacific Northwest city focusing on social justice. For more than eight months and counting, the city has experienced anarchy. Some thought it would end when President Biden came to office, but BLM activists marched through the city on inauguration day smashing windows and holding a banner that said: "We Don't Want Biden: We Want Revenge and chanting "No good cop, no good president! Black Lives Matter!" [342] In an interview, Portland's white leftist Mayor Ted Wheeler was asked about "the city and its residents being held hostage by a few hundred people." He said, "they're right. They're absolutely right." In 2021, when Wheeler attempted to get tough on lawlessness, he found that his long-term alliance with the city's subjugators cast him as their puppet. Activists tracked him down, and one woman punched him in the face. Naturally, he didn't press charges. In the same interview, Wheeler said, "we have to make a good faith effort to at least demonstrate that we understand, that policing generally has led to the deaths of too many black people, especially black men." [343] In 2020, in total, Portland police killed two white men. In 2019 it was 4 white men, 1 black and 1 Latino. In 2018, 5 white men, 1 white woman, and 1 black man. In 2017, 3 black and 3 white and in 2016, 3 white. In 2015 it was 6 white.[344] All were a justified use of force. Obviously, Portland doesn't have a problem with police killing black people. So, why would Wheeler allow Portland to be held hostage? To burnish his social justice bona fides? Or was this part of a master plan by the Democratic Party to leverage violence to open veins of spending for constituents?

Across the country, states are decriminalizing marijuana. One impetus is to reduce the arrests of blacks for non-violent crimes. In 2018 drug arrests for possession ensnared 1.42 million people, including 383,000 blacks. Half of the arrests were for marijuana possession.[345] California took the lead in tackling this issue with the oddly named Safe Neighborhoods and Schools Act of 2014. This virtually made it legal to use illegal drugs. One inadvertent outcome has been to encourage people to shoot up in public, which is bad for tourism, public safety, and for the prying eyes of school children. Felonies for drug convictions have though been reduced, and that was the goal. In 2021, Oregon assumed the lead when it implemented a law to decriminalize the possession of drugs. The motive was to reduce drug-related convictions for blacks. A report produced for the period 2016-17 found a population that is 85% white accounted for 83% of drug-related convictions. Meanwhile, a black population of 1.9% accounted for 3.6% of convictions. In 2018 this dropped to 2.9 percent.[346]

Oregon's law has been championed around the country for tackling racial disparities in drug-related offenses. It seems sensible to limit arrests and criminal records for drugs (marijuana) that are sold legally in 72% of states for medical or recreational purposes. In Oregon, these arrests are not for recreational use of marijuana because that is legal and has been for small amounts since 1973. They have been for possession of other drugs and drug dealing. The quantities of drugs permitted in the new law are sufficient to enable small drug dealers to stay employed legally. For example, it's legal to possess enough heroine to kill 30 people, or 40 pills of oxycodone of any strength. It's possible they will have to grapple with how to prosecute a legal drug dealer that peddles deadly dope. In 2020, 580 people overdosed on drugs in Oregon, and most had ingested drugs including heroine and oxycodone laced with fentanyl.[347] Another issue that should be on the radar is the fact that "the more accessible a drug is, the greater the likelihood that someone will pick it up."[348] Heroin, cocaine, and methamphetamine count among the most addictive drugs and these are now legal to possess and buy from small-time dealers. Finally, as grand social justice champions, they may have to contemplate the issue of making sure drug pushers make the minimum wage. One study showed that the guy or gal on the street would make more money working at a fast-food restaurant. [349]

Oregon may not know that this law is depriving some blacks of a badge of honor because blacks see going to prison for supplying a product that people want as unjust and as a badge of strength. "The ex-con is a hero rather than someone who went the wrong way." Blacks are victims of an unjust law targeting victimless crimes. [350] Victimless, unless the dope peddled proves lethal, people become addicted and do horrible things, or people on dope kill or maim someone. Oregon won't actually be depriving many blacks of a badge of strength, because not many blacks are arrested or convicted for drug-related offenses. About 145 blacks were convicted in 2018. [351] This is more like a social justice-oriented law for smaller drug pushers of all races. At what cost? Will the people of Oregon find an increase in people shooting up in public, people overdosed on the street, increases in property crime, and drug transactions conducted in open view of their children? Of course. Will that impede business in downtown areas, like Portland, of course. There will, however, be far fewer drug-related convictions, and of course social justice for small-time drug dealers.

Disproportional commission of crimes. In the United States, how disproportional is the commission of crimes or arrests for crimes? Whites and non-black Latinos grouped together form 73% of the population. Blacks are 13.4% and Asians 5.6%. In 2019, 41% of murders were committed by whites and white Latinos, 56% by blacks, and 1.5% by Asians. Sixty percent of murders by juveniles (<18) were committed by blacks and 38% by whites and white Latinos.[352],[xxviii] Arrests for robberies were 45% for whites and white Latinos, 53% for blacks, and 1.5% for Asians. Arrests for drug-related offenses were 71% white, 26% black, and 1.3% Asian. The one crime that is pretty proportional to the population is driving under the influence, although Asians were still low at 2.6%.[353]

To keep criminal convictions proportional to their populations, instead of tackling crime and the drivers of crime, the solution is increasingly to legalize it, but only for the

---

[xxviii] Juveniles committed 7% of all murders in both racial groups.

populations committing too much crime. In California a law became effective January 1, 2021, that should make people's hair stand on end. This law makes it impossible to charge a person with a crime (even if certifiably guilty) "if there is statistical evidence that people of one race are disproportionately charged or convicted of a specific crime or enhancement." [354] The people that will benefit from this law are blacks and Latinos, including gang bangers, because they disproportionately commit crime in California, including violent crime. [355] This law promises to deliver social justice for many blacks and Latinos, including the gang bangers.

All of these legalization-of-crime solutions deliver social justice for the so-called victims of an unjust society. For the actual crime victims, there is no justice. These solutions are encouraging more crime and converting cities from enjoyable places to stroll, shop and dine into dangerous areas that scream keep out. This won't have favorable social or economic outcomes. Seems like politicians are making this tradeoff to achieve equity with respect to criminal convictions.

Social justice and sanctuary cities. Sanctuary cities "protect" undocumented people from the reach of the Federal Immigration and Customs Enforcement Agency (ICE). In theory, sanctuary cities are only supposed to "protect" undocumented immigrants from prosecution for misdemeanors, but there are many examples of felonies, including murder where an undocumented person was given a get out jail free card and allowed to stay in the United States. This is social justice for undocumenteds and no justice for their victims.

The sanctuary city argument is that undocumented people are basically law abiding and should be given leniency. Sending someone back to their homeland is seen as cruel and unusual punishment -- not social justice. Back home these scofflaws committing a similar crime could be locked up for a long time. The law-abiding argument is unsupported by the data. Crime data for undocumenteds has become hard to find because so many are never charged, but when data was collected in 2004, 95% of outstanding arrest warrants for homicide and two-thirds of fugitive felony warrants in Los Angeles were for undocumenteds. [356] When it comes to federal crimes, a report in 2019 showed undocumenteds "accounted for 24 percent of all federal drug arrests, 25 percent of all federal property arrests, and 28 percent of all federal fraud arrests…In 2018, a quarter of all federal drug arrests took place in the five judicial districts along the U.S.-Mexico border." Considering that undocumenteds make up 3% of the population, these are pretty impressive crime statistics. [357] People in California complaining about the extra crime motivated by special treatment for undocumenteds were cast as racist and anti-immigrant. [358]

Social justice advocates, which include a host of bureaucrats and elected officials are skilled at mangling data and the rights of undocumented people with immigrants that are here legally. When they defend sanctuary cities, they can intentionally group legal and illegal alike and ascribe the protected freedoms that are available to the latter to the former. This is an easy sell in a nation where most people can't name the three branches of government.[359] In 2021, the mangling of data on legal immigrants and undocumenteds is becoming the norm. The word alien, which means a person from a foreign country, and is most often used in the form illegal alien, also known as undocumented, is being removed from the legal lexicon. The new word is noncitizen, but this includes legal immigrants and undocumenteds. Now when someone speaks about the need to control the borders, they will reflexively have to endure the racist slur for being anti-immigrant (anti-noncitizens). This may not be happenstance.

There is a close relationship between sanctuary cities, undocumenteds, and the Democratic Party. Sanctuary cities are blue state creations that surfaced during the rise of legal and illegal Latino immigrants. Enforcing immigration laws risks Latino voter allegiance to the party. In the words of police leaders, who insisted on anonymity: "People are afraid of a backlash from Hispanics." "I would get a firestorm of criticism if I talked about [enforcing the immigration law against illegals]." At what cost do these votes come? According to Patrick Ortega of Radio Nueva Vida: "Institutionalizing illegal immigration creates a mindset in people that anything goes in the U.S…It creates a new subculture, with a sequel of social ills." This coincides with 30-80 percent of released undocumenteds being reoffenders, and with the severity of crimes often escalating. Between 2010 and 2016 re-offenders committed 130 murders. It seems the law-abiding undocumented narrative is seriously flawed. Then again it may have been true when the punishment for an undocumented committing crime was deportation. Now they are primed for creating a sequel of social ills .[360,361,362]

Protecting national borders. Every sovereign nation must control who can travel across and live within its borders. The day a nation stops protecting its borders is the day a nation jeopardizes national security and the safety of its citizens. The various statistics on crimes committed by undocumenteds that was just noted tells a compelling story for controlling our nation's borders Also useful is knowing that in 2018, 2,028 were murdered and in 2019, 1,923 were murdered by noncitizens, which include undocumenteds and legal immigrants who have not become naturalized citizens. This was about 13% of all murders during these years. Noncitizens make up 7% of the population. [363,364]

The border with Mexico is where most undocumenteds enter the United States. Most fentanyl trafficked into the United States comes from the southern border. In 2019, ICE seized enough fentanyl to poison every American. [365] Drug trafficking is a big reason undocumenteds are over-represented in federal drug arrests. Undocumenteds were 16% of all drug traffickers arrested in 2018 (undocumenteds are 3% of the population).[366] Half of all deaths due to drug overdoses in 2019, about 35,000, were tied to fentanyl. In 2020, it was about 48,000. Whites have been disproportionately dying from drug overdoses. This led many to sound off that controlling the border to limit drug trafficking was an act of white privilege. This was followed by a demand that the nation instead focus on social justice for people illegally entering the country. The advocates have won. They may relish a victory over white privilege, but blacks are now dying proportionately to their population from fentanyl and opioid overdoses. With more fentanyl coming across the border, blacks may soon be dying disproportionately from drug overdoses, too. [367,368,369,370] It seems like there are a lot of ways that social justice can backfire.

It's not just drugs that are smuggled across the border. The southern border is home to a $7 billion industry in human smuggling, and one expected to become larger in 2021. This is because the border wall has been halted and there is a new policy that allows illegally smuggled people to stay in the United States if they have criminal records for "drug crimes (less serious offenses), simple assault, DUI, money laundering, property crimes, fraud, tax crimes, solicitation, or charges without convictions."[371] Naturally, once they reside here, they can find sanctuary to continue committing crime. Democratic politicians and much of the media has been in favor of opening up the southern border. Issues related to the pandemic have been sidelined.

African American PBS commentator, Yamiche Alcindor, called America's policies on controlling illegal immigration at the southern border an act of white supremacists targeting brown people, and suggested reparations for illegal immigrants that are not treated with social justice. [372] Alcindor was mistaken about the brown people, because most are white, but that dilutes the white supremacy accusation and makes social justice advocacy harder to rationalize. She may also be uninformed about the extremely prejudicial environments against blacks that these new Latinos hail from. While white supremacy died in the United States in the late 1960s and early 1970s, anti-racism is not a theme in Latin America. In Ecuador, the targeting of blacks by police is a formal part of their jobs. The police "conceive of their mission as protecting citizens from the 'danger' of blacks. These blacks are not viewed as citizens but rather as violent intruders that invade the cities." [373,xxix] In other nations, blacks believe the police think it is their job to physically mistreat them. [374] Blacks were legally prohibited from immigrating to El Salvador from 1933 to the 1980s. In 2019, Brazilian police in one city, Rio de Janeiro, killed over 1,400 black people.[375] These new measures to encourage illegal immigration, could also result in social justice backfiring.

In 2017, former President Trump per his charter attempted to protect the nation from additional acts of terror. In doing this, he limited travel to the United States from Iran, Iraq, Libya, Somalia, Sudan, Syria, and Yemen. Just two years earlier, President Obama, per his charter, had a similar ban on the same countries. The ban affected seven out of 49 Muslim-majority nations. All of these nations had problems with airport screenings, and they had serious issues with terrorism within their borders. The University of Maryland's Global Terrorism Database has records of terrorist attacks in these nations that number 600 for Iran, 68,500 for Iraq, 2,300 for Libya, 4,600 for Somalia, 900 for Sudan, 2,450 for Syria and 3,600 for Yemen. The 2017 ban was dubbed the Muslim ban and it met widespread protests with cries of racism against Muslims, even though some of these nations have Christian, Jewish and other religious populations, and only 14% of Muslim-majority nations and 12% of Muslims were affected.

Democratic Socialist Congresswoman and Somali American Ilhan Omar called the ban hateful, xenophobic, a divider of families, an obstructor of dreams, and a killer of religious freedom. [376] Omar knows a bit about xenophobia and killing religious freedoms. Her homeland is 99+% Muslim and has 0% white people. She obviously cannot know that Muslim terrorists have obstructed American dreams. She characterized 9/11 as "some people did something." Coming from a country with 4,600 terrorist attacks, perhaps nonchalance sets in. So much so, someone can think, like Omar does that the discrimination faced by Muslim Americans after 9/11 is no different than the Muslim discrimination faced by the thousands murdered on 9/11. She has shown sympathy for Muslim terrorists, and she seeks and has sought equity solutions for Muslims, including Muslim terrorists. Hear! Hear! Social justice for terrorists. Being a black Muslim woman seems to work in her favor. A white person seeking leniency for Klansmen would not get a pass. Who has privilege now?

[xxix] In early America, police forces targeted "dangerous classes." These were blacks, foreign immigrants (mostly Irish and Italian), and the poor.

Have we reached a point where national leaders will face rancorous uninformed social justice advocates, including some state and local political leaders that are happy to sacrifice national security and the safety of citizens and property by twisted obsessions with racism, equity, and social justice?

The illusion of racist cops. A comprehensive study on police shootings overseen by African American Harvard Professor Roland Fryer in 2016 found no racial bias by white police toward blacks. The study found that unarmed blacks are no more likely to die at the hands of white police officers than unarmed whites. Black officers were, however found more likely to kill unarmed whites than white officers. A 2019 study published by the National Academy of Sciences also found no evidence of racial disparities in police shootings. [377,378,xxx] In America today, data does not interfere with "good stories" like the one carefully cultivated to dismantle the police and do undo harm to public safety. Real data are buried beneath one-sided presentations of a black person that has been killed by police that grab and hold the headlines for weeks. A survey from 2020 found that 44% of people self-categorizing as liberal or very liberal thought more than 1,000 unarmed black men had been killed by police in 2019. About a quarter thought it was 10,000 or more. The number was fourteen. People of all political orientations overestimated the percentage of blacks killed by police. Conservatives were the lowest with 37.8%. Liberals and very liberals estimated 56.16% and 60.4% respectively. The percentage was 22.6%. [379] The numerous headlines reporting an epidemic of police killings of black people or any people is also unsupported by 0.0014% of police involved in fatal shootings. [380]

How can 0.0014% be correct? What about all those bad apples on the police force that everyone talks about? Between 2005 and 2019, 104 on-duty police officers were arrested and charged with the unnecessary use of force that resulted in a murder or manslaughter. Thirty-five were convicted. Based on a police force of 700,000, on an annual basis, that puts the potential police bad apples at 0.0001% and the convicted bad apples at 0.000003% of the police force. [381] In 2020, this translates into 146 cops being killed by criminals for every bad apple cop. Looks like the criminals are winning the war on cops.

It's very very very infrequent that a person engaging in criminal activity would be killed by a police officer. Police use force when they believe a suspect poses an immediate threat to them or others, or when suspects are actively evading arrest. That's obviously not what people think. During a BLM protest in Rochester, NY, there was an exchange between white and black BLM activists. "White folks, allies, accomplices, I'm talking to you all. This is not a video game. For some of you all that come here, you come because it's an elective. We come because it's survival." It was around this time that article headlines blasted blacks three times more likely than whites to be killed by police. [382] It may be three times more likely (it was 2.3 times in 2020), but it's not at all likely. Of all crimes committed in the United States in 2019, only about half of the people are arrested. In one year, of those that were arrested, 1 in 10,095 ended up being killed by police. For a black person the probability was 1 in 11,801 and for whites 1 in 16,237. (In 2019, blacks were arrested about 2.2 times for all crimes, 3.7 times for violent crimes and 5.2 times for murder than whites.) The chance for an unarmed black man engaging in crime being killed by police in 2019 was 0.000525%. The chance of an unarmed black man engaging in crime that doesn't seriously threaten the police being killed by police was 0.00022%. Looking at

---

[xxx] The study also showed that blacks and Latinos were more likely to experience non-lethal force by police, but a direct correlation to race rather than other factors, i.e., criminal record and resisting arrest, could not be determined.

total crimes rather than arrests halves this percentages to 0.00011%. The chance of being struck by lightning is 0.00020%.[383] If blacks want to improve survivability when it comes to the police, the best bet is to forego engaging in criminal activity. Then the probability of being killed by a police officer is zero.

This is something else that people obviously wouldn't think. The probability of a policeman being killed by a civilian is much higher than a policeman killing someone engaged in a crime. Based on 2020 line-of-duty killings, the probability of an officer being killed in one year was 0.048% or about 5 times higher than a policeman killing a person engaged in a crime. [384,385]

There were 999 fatal police shootings in 2020. No data is available for 2020 but in 2019 about 3-4% of victims were unarmed or armed with something like a stun gun or a moving vehicle. The unarmed included 14 black men and 25 white men. Of the 14 black men, eight threatened the police with force.[386,xxxi] The small number/percentage of unarmed black men that were killed, may surprise some. People are more likely to hear things like African American Senator Cory Booker say that *mostly* unarmed black men are being murdered by police officers. When did 6% or 3% if you eliminate those that seriously threatened police, become mostly? It's also important to note that the 3% or 6% were being pursued for a crime when they were shot. [387]

Criminal behavior drives police behavior. It's not unusual for social justice advocates to pillory cops as racists whenever they see an unequal power situation between cops and criminals. Police are never given the benefit of the doubt and people dismiss the reality that officer behavior is driven by civilian behavior. Cops are trained not to take out their weapons unless they feel it is necessary. For example, if someone were to attack them. African American Angela Rye, a political commentator for CNN advised black viewers to fight the police. She said, "every time we don't fight back, we die." [388] Rye was parroting some often-heard propaganda and giving really bad advice. Fighting with police would certainly provoke use of force, but in general refusing police requests, for example, to keep your hands visible can make police leery. Still, the use of a weapon is very infrequent and so is the use of force.

Many African American children are taught or learn to code switch between the African American Vernacular and standard English. Code switching is though more than just shifting to standard English and includes using good manners, keeping your hands visible, not slouching and turning down loud music. [389,390] I suspect most white children have been taught similar things to show respect to all people in authority and they do it without code switching. Evidently, that's because it's part of "white culture," although apparently its part of Asian and Latino culture too. When it comes to police, these non-black children may show respect because it's a sensible way to avoid risking an unpleasant encounter with a police officer that will be suspicious of people with suspicious behaviors, like someone keeping their hands hidden, or not responding to police requests because they can't hear them. Police are afraid of dying too, and they are 5 times more likely to be killed while pursuing criminals than criminals are when engaging with police.

Policing and social justice. Delegitimizing the police and gaining support for defunding the police has been made simple with the use of technology. It's become common when police get near a black person for people to take out their cell phones and start recording. Should a black person be shot by a police officer, edited footage will be

---

xxxi Data analyzing the deaths of unarmed white people was not available.

posted on social media and then picked up by the mainstream media. Now, the nation has another cause célèbre accompanied by a loud chorus of systemically racist America and racist cops, and the nation is thrown into turmoil. The police who have rules on what they can release after an incident are relatively defenseless. In 2020 the police killed 432 whites, 226 blacks, 156 Latinos, and 185 others.[391] Does anyone remember the media covering a white, Latino or other, being shot by the police? Senior Fellow at the Hoover Institute, Shelby Steele said that the blacks are the only community that demand justice for people behaving badly. Blacks are, after all, victims. (When self-proclaimed victims behave aggressively, they see their behaviors as a rational response to being a victim of oppression.) The demands for justice have been working, minimally in the news. Sometimes in cash payments and sometimes in court. Remember crowds of cheering black people when OJ Simpson was acquitted after the evidence seemed incontrovertible that he had brutally murdered his white wife and her white Jewish friend. Simpson didn't indicate any affection for black people, but he was a black hero and a black victim. African American California Congresswoman Maxine Waters demanded that the black men that nearly murdered a white truck driver in 1992 be given "justice." If not, "we're going to have a civil war." The attempted murder actually occurred within a civil war that saw black people rip light-skinned people from their cars. Tension between Asian and black communities motivated targeting the destruction of businesses owned by Koreans and other Asians. Arson-ignited infernos blazed in parts of Los Angeles. Waters saw these black men and the rioters as heroes. They were settling a score for the acquittal of white and Latino police officers charged with using excessive force on a black man. Quite unusually for its time, the exchange was filmed.

Blacks demanding justice for people whose behaviors are criminal, suspect, or dismissive of complying with police, is part one. The second part is making them heroes. The latest hero is George Floyd. Between 1997 and 2005 George Floyd was imprisoned eight times. In his last encounter with the police, he was high on fentanyl and was trying to use counterfeit money. [392] He was resisting arrest and police struggled to restrain him. The Hennepin County Medical Examiner Andrew Baker told prosecutors that absent other apparent causes of death, it "could be acceptable" to rule the death an overdose, based on the level of fentanyl in Floyd's system." [393] The apparent cause of death that Baker references is excessive use of force by the police. Floyd didn't deserve to die from a policeman using a knee-on-neck hold, but did he deserve four funeral services and a gold coffin that was carried by a horse drawn carriage? It was a funeral usually reserved for heads of state. There were a few other cause célèbre that filled the airwaves in 2020. Some were resisting arrest and some involved arms. All of them became heroes. People bought T-shirts with their pictures, football players kneeled for social justice during the "white" National Anthem and had images of the fallen heroes on their helmets. All the images were of black people. None of the whites, Asians or others that had been killed by police became heroes. These displays supporting social justice were an important part of the movements to defund police.

Is it blacks motivating the media or has the media gotten in on making heroes out of people behaving badly? The media lionized both Jacob Blake and his father, and they still do. According to the investigation undertaken by Kenosha County, on August 23, 2020, police were responding to a domestic violence call made by Blake's ex-girlfriend. Blake already had an outstanding warrant for domestic violence. When police tried to arrest

Blake, he resisted and managed to put one cop in a headlock. When he was shot by police, he was armed with a knife. On August 27, 2020, Kamala Harris made her position clear; Blake was a victim of racist cops. "I don't see how anybody could reason that that was justifiable… the officer should be charged… We have had too many Black men in America who have been the subject of this kind of conduct." BLM activists calling to defund the police wrapped Kenosha, Wisconsin in unrest for four more days. BLM activists predicted the city would burn until there was justice, and it did. In total there was $50 million in property damage. Candidates Joe Biden and Kamala Harris traveled independently to meet with Blake. Harris told him "she was…proud of him and how he is working through his pain." Biden met with the family and praised their resilience and optimism. Blake's father is a known racist and vile anti-Semite. Biden told the people of Kenosha, as president he was going to fix the "original sin of the country," slavery. Blake Jr. and Blake Sr. both became heroes. Victims of racist cops and slavery, no? Meanwhile, Harris and Biden have become the latest White House champions of the war on cops.[394, 395,396,397,398]

Defund the police. The defund the police movement has been motivated by the narrative of racist cops – racist killer cops. In reality, blacks have been waging a war on cops for a long time. It's not just because blacks disproportionately engage in crime and consequently disproportionately encounter police, apparently it also ties to a belief that "American police forces were established to catch fugitive slaves and have acted as the guardians of white supremacy ever since." "The slave patrols should be considered a forerunner of modern American law enforcement."[399] Black Lives Matter promotes that policing and police violence is a product of "white folks taught to fear Black folks." [400] According to African American lawyer, Malaika Jabali, "policing in America was never created to protect and serve the masses. It can't be reformed because it is designed for violence." [401] The original sin of slavery and its follow-on endemic racism strikes again. It would seem prudent for people that promote and impose anti-policing views based on 18th and 19th century policing to look at policing today.

The real driver for defunding the police is more likely to be a hatred of police. While 64% of Americans like the police, 64% of blacks do not.[402] Blacks tend to frame disproportional run ins with the law as racist. But there is no evidence of systemic racism in policing. It would not be absurd to think that police unconsciously know that blacks are 3.2 times more likely to kill a cop than a white person, but even here, there is no evidence that this results in discriminatory actions.

Policing in America has been evolving for 150 years in response to current demands for law and order, racial justice, and community outreach. This has been taking place within the rough and tumble world of police fighting crime to keep America's long list of protected freedoms safe. Or at least that's what they used to do before laws became arbitrary and pimps and hustlers, like BLM activists, largely succeeded in reversing the good guy, bad guy roles for police officers and criminals.

Defund the police movements, non-stop taunting of police, and a 57% increase in police line-of-duty deaths in 2020 has reasonably led to less active policing. [403] For police, it's too risky to engage in high crime neighborhoods and particularly black neighborhoods. It's not just getting killed, no policeman wants to be on the national news compliments of an edited or one-sided cell phone video. Cell phones are everywhere and no matter what the police are doing in black communities it's a lose lose situation. Police are marked and markings are made sharper when celebrities like 6'9" and 250-pound LeBron James tweets to his 66 million followers that he is afraid to go outside because he is "literally hunted every day," and we are not talking about paparazzi. An unarmed man of any color going about his business being hunted down doesn't pass the sniff test. Even accepting that $39 million-a-year LeBron James is a victim of white oppression, the chance of a person of any color minding his or her own business being killed by police is zero.

The ones that suffer the most from a reduction in active policing are blacks, because it is their communities where crime is highest, and police are tasked to work in the highest crime areas. Blacks are 23% of the population of NYC and responsible for 75% of shootings and 70% of robberies. Blacks and Latinos account for 98% of the shootings. Whites are 33% of the population and responsible for 2% of the shootings and 4% of the robberies. In Chicago, blacks are 30% of the population and responsible for 80% of shootings. Forty-seven percent of black men between the ages of 20 and 24 neither work nor go to school. Whites are 33% of the populations, and they commit 1% of shootings. [404] Within these cities, black crime is mostly committed in black neighborhoods, much as white crime is mostly committed in white neighborhoods.

There has been a steep rise in violent crime since police ratcheted down their active policing. In 2020, fifty-one US cities saw an increase in homicides of 35% or more. Homicides were up 15% in Detroit, 10% in Washington DC, 25% in NY, Philadelphia 39%, and Chicago 56%. The number murdered in Chicago is close to the total number of fatal police shootings in the United States in 2020. An assessment in June 2020 found that in Chicago there was one non-police-related homicide every 15 hours. In 6-months police killed three people.[405] By year end, seventy-nine Chicago police had been shot at. That was four times as many as in 2019.[406] In the five cities just noted most murders and murderers were black. About 90% of blacks that are murdered, are murdered by blacks.[xxxii] The murders include hundreds of black juveniles.[xxxiii, 407, 408, 409] Manhattan Institute Senior Fellow, Heather McDonald has really tried to draw attention to the severe problem of blacks killing blacks, and asking why is it that black lives only matter when a black person is killed by a cop. [410] In the movie Uncle Tom, it was asked why do blacks spend so much time recalling the KKK when blacks kill more blacks in one year than the KKK did in 70 years? [411] The answer to both questions is the same. Keeping whites on the hook and blacks as blameless victims.

Defunding initiatives may point to more homicides for blacks. A study on policing in the United States concluded that "our estimates suggest that 'defunding' the police could result in more deaths, especially among black Americans." [412] This may be one reason why gun sales to African Americans increased 58% in 2020.[413] It may also be the reason 81% of blacks said they don't want less police, and some said they want more, despite the movement to defund the police.[414]

Tackling crime rather than police. Police tackle crime -- not race. Disproportional run ins are due to disproportional crime. Why are blacks disproportionately arrested for crime? Because they commit more crime and police are in their neighborhoods trying to control crime. If some arrests are being influenced by the presence of police in high crime areas, there is a cure for that. Reduce crime. Police have to prioritize their time and low crime neighborhoods don't make the cut. Why do blacks commit more crime? Some

---

[xxxii] Eighty-eight percent of whites are killed by whites.
[xxxiii] The final tally of black juveniles murdered by blacks in 2020 is not yet available. In 2019 the number was 544.

contributors include minimum wage laws, devaluing education, attractiveness of gang membership, residential choices, badges of honor, and a cult of victimology. Some of this can be tied to children being raised without a father being five time more likely to engage in crime. Fathers can be very influential in keeping children from engaging in crime, although fathers that are ex-cons can present mixed messages.[415,416]

Parents jointly raising their children is the most effective way to tackle poverty and reduce crime and incarcerations. Politicians are loathed to put emphasis on this solution. They seem unwilling to even tinker with government assistance programs that inadvertently motivate and reward single parent households. Black leaders seem to have given up on this message too. When Obama tried, he was called an Uncle Tom. Non-black politicians would be called racists. The premier organization for blacks today is Black Lives Matter and they do not support nuclear families. Somewhere along the way, nuclear families became associated with white culture. Nuclear families are also part of Asian American culture. Actually, there is a preference for nuclear two-parent families in almost every nation/culture in the world. [417] For all races everywhere, a father at home and helping to raise children can do a world of good. "Children who grow up without a father are five times more likely to live in poverty and commit crime; nine times more likely to drop out of schools and twenty times more likely to end up in prison." Just in case someone should see that the crime to prison ratio is different in the above quote, prison is more likely for violent crimes, and blacks disproportionately engage in violent crime.

"What makes this Nation different is our respect for and adherence to the law because the law is the greatest unifying force in our culture, and it is the great equalizing force in our culture."[418] Everyone is equal in the eyes of the law. Not anymore. For the so-called victims of oppression or whatever, we have social justice. Steal if you must; sell dope if you like; riot when displeased with perceived injustice; disrespect the police; and enter our country illegally, and you will be rewarded with a lifestyle better than where you came and you will have special civil rights unavailable to most citizens. Social justice is a euphemism for sticking it to the so-called people of privilege. Newly woke people are turning so-called "victims" into the new oppressors that can break into the cars and homes of "people of privilege" without recourse. Is it any wonder that gun sales in America have gone through the roof? Legal gun sales were up 40% in 2020 (40 million sold) and they are poised for an even bigger rise in 2021. [419] America has entered a very dangerous period where rule of law is being sacrificed for an ill-defined notion of social justice that is predicated on hype, ignorance, and misguided guilt. This, we are told is equity. Equity is nothing more than legalizing discrimination against people who obey the rule of law, work hard, and are self-reliant. These are the new scofflaws.

We live in a crazy time where statues of Ulysses S Grant and Abraham Lincoln have been torn down. Both American heroes have been cancelled. In 21st century America it's not enough that Lincoln issued a presidential order to free the slaves, was the commander overseeing a civil war to end slavery and died for his position on voting rights for blacks. You see his conviction on racial equality was not strong enough. Today, Lincoln has become a disappointment. General Ulysses S. Grant led the Union army to victory, and he was a committed anti-racist. As president he destroyed the KKK and championed black voting rights. He had a slave that he freed at the start of the Civil War, and his record with Native Americans is checkered. He too, must be cancelled from history and his statues removed. If only these historical heroes had the unblemished records of extraordinary achievements like our new heroes. George Floyd will have a permanent monument in Minneapolis. Lincoln is cancelled and Floyd is his replacement. It's all under America's Big Top.

The Non-Racist Medical Profession and System

Disproportionate outcomes in healthcare are regularly wrongly attributed to racist doctors and racism in health care. BLM has a separate movement called White Coats for Black Lives that has demanded America acknowledge that health disparities are due to racism. To support racism in healthcare there are normative statements, anecdotes, surveys, reports on the disproportional presence of some diseases, disproportional deaths from disease, powerful personal stories, and perceptions of discrimination.[420] In 2017, the Robert Wood Johnson Foundation found that 32% of African Americans have perceived discrimination in health care. Latino Americans and Asian Americans have also perceived discrimination in healthcare, and to a lesser degree, whites.

Outside perceptions, personal stories, and mostly normative statements, data does not support a racist medical profession. Doctors are sworn to treat all patients equally. They are concerned with diseases and other maladies -- not race. Do they provide services congenially? There is plenty of support for doctors having a god complex and "bad bedside" manner. Doctors also tend to have very hectic schedules. Both of these factors can lead patients to feel like they aren't being treated without respect (treated inferior) or not being given the attention they might like and perceive others getting. Thirty-seven percent of black women say in the last year a doctor has talked down to them and 41% said they were treated disrespectfully. For black men the percentages were 15% and 17% respectively. Ninety-four percent of doctors are non-black, which could easily inspire perceptions of disrespect and racism. [421,xxxiv] Minorities perceiving more discrimination is also consistent with research that shows "minorities may less often than majorities view contact situations as involving equal status." [422]

This chapter reviews a number of areas where racism has been alleged in healthcare, including infant mortality, pain management, disproportionate health outcomes, Covid-19 deaths, flu-related deaths, and the disproportionate presence of doctors by race. The data-based findings in this chapter are unsupportive of a racist health care system or racist doctors. It is supportive of some groups disproportionately engaging in unhealthy behaviors from poor eating habits to insufficient exercise, ignoring the advice of medical providers, and being remiss with preventive health measures.

A very troubling disparity in healthcare relates to infant mortality. Black babies die at a rate that is 2.1 times higher than whites. One report in 2020 showed a lower mortality rate when black pregnant mothers were treated by black doctors. The media presented this as proof of racist doctors. But it does not prove this. Black patients are likely to see non-black doctors as talking down to them (94% are non-black), but this is less so with black doctors. Black patients are more likely to trust black doctors and to develop a good rapport. Blacks are also more likely to follow their advice and take prescribed medicines. Many students in med school have been told not to be surprised if blacks don't trust non-black doctors. The problem for blacks is that ignoring the advice of a doctor could certainly influence health outcomes, and in this case the life of a baby. When it comes to lessening infant mortality, there are a number of other influential factors including the mother's education and lifestyle, marital status, and access to health care. It's been noted that blacks, more than any other group have lower educational outcomes. The educational level of a pregnant woman or any person has a significant impact on health outcomes and longevity because it

---

xxxiv The ethnicity of 13.7% of physicians was unknown.

has been proven to influence adopting a healthy lifestyle. Education also has a role that can reduce deaths from Sudden Unexpected Infant Death Syndrome (SUID), which includes deaths from Sudden Infant Death Syndrome (SIDs). Material reductions have occurred in SUIDs when mothers gain familiarity and adhere to the recommendations for safe sleeping patterns. African American mothers more than any other racial group have been less likely to adhere to these recommendations. Annually, SUIDs account for about 17% of all infant mortality. Death by SUIDs is from 2-6 times higher for African Americans than whites, Latinos, and Asians. [423,424]

Black women are also much less likely to be married. Marriage, at least a good marriage, has a positive effect on happiness and this influences health. Black women are also less likely to exercise. Exercising has an enormous impact on health. When it comes to a healthy lifestyle, a healthy weight is important. Infant mortality has been reported from 1.57 to 2 times higher when women are obese. Another study found that 61% of infants that died had mothers that were overweight (25%) or obese (35.7%). Overweight mothers accounted for about 30% of all infant mortality deaths. An estimated 80.6% of black women are overweight vs. 64.8% of white women.[425,426, 427,428] Black women are alone in being disproportionately overweight and obese. Blacks are 13.4% of the population. Black women are 22% of the obese and 28% of the overweight population of women. For Latinas the numbers are 18.5% of the population, 22% obese and 13.4% overweight. For white women it is 60% of the population, 52% obese and 45% overweight, and Asian women 5.6% of the population, 1.5% obese, and 5.5% of the overweight female population.[429] Infant mortality is also much higher for girls 15-19 (30% higher) and highest for girls under 15 (300% higher), compared to women that are 25-39.[xxxv] In both groups, blacks and Latinas are disproportionately present.[xxxvi,430,431]

Shifting to healthcare in the general population, disproportionate health outcomes are pointed to as proof of racism. No more data is needed than a 2019 study that found black people aged 51–55 were 28% more likely to already have a chronic illness compared to white people of the same age.[432] To support an accusation of racism, it is best that there is no more data because there is plenty to support that different health outcomes are due to individual behaviors and not racism. Increasingly poor health outcomes, generally, are tied to increasingly sedentary lifestyles and its relationship to being overweight. A study between 1988 and 2010 found the number of women reporting no physical activity jumped from 19% to 52%. For men it was 11% and 42%.[xxxvii,433]

The percent of people in different racial groups that meet the CDC's exercise guidelines are low across races/ethnicities, but lowest among blacks and Native Americans. For whites, the percent meeting guidelines was 25.7%, Asians 22.9%, Latinos 21.4%, blacks 19.9%, and Native Americans 19.1%.[434,xxxviii] One reason African American women do not exercise according to African American US Surgeon General Regina Benjamin (2009-2013) is that certain hairstyles don't do well with sweat or additional washing. Rationales notwithstanding, a sedentary lifestyle accelerates nearly every unwanted aspect of age-related medical disorders. The correlations between exercising at the recommended levels and reduced health care outcomes is overwhelming. There are 30-

---

[xxxv] Mothers at these ages are 0.1% (<15) and 8% (16-19) of the population of mothers.

[xxxvi] Twenty-three percent of mothers (15-19) and 34% of mothers (<15) were blacks and 34% of mothers (15-19) and 38% of mothers (<15) were Latinas.

[xxxvii] The increase in obesity during this time was 10% for women and 15% for men.

[xxxviii] The recommended amount of exercise is from 150-300 minutes per week or from 75-150 vigorous minutes.

50% reductions in depression, reductions up to 50% in osteoarthritis, reductions of 25-50% in cardiovascular deaths, and reductions in chronic pain, hypertension, colon cancer, hip fractures, chronic fatigue, obesity, and diabetes. [435,436,437,438,439,440]

Exercise decreased and obesity increased. From 1999 to 2018, the prevalence of obesity in America increased from 30.5% to 42.4%, and the prevalence of severe obesity increased from 4.7% to 9.2%. [441] Being overweight is the single greatest contributing factor to an increased presence of diseases and other unfavorable health outcomes. The more overweight, the worse the outcomes. America's obesity trend is a major contributing factor to diminished health outcomes across races/ethnicities, but blacks and Native Americans are hit especially hard because these populations are the most disproportionately overweight. Culturally, blacks don't subscribe to thin is in and they are more likely to be overweight, obese, and severely obese. The black culture generally accepts "larger body sizes and feels less guilty about overeating than other ethnic groups." [442] Blacks are 13.4% of the population but 25% of the overweight, 19% of the obese, and 22% of the severely obese population. Latinos are 18.5% of the population, 15% of the overweight, 21% of the obese, and 18% of the severely obese population. Whites are 60% of the population, 52% of the overweight, 55% of the obese, and 64% of the severely obese population. Asians are 5.6% of the population and 5.5% of the overweight, 2.1% of the obese, and 1.4% of the severely obese population. Native Americans are 1.2% of the population and 7.6% of the overweight population.[443,444,445,446,xxxix] According to Project 1619, if there was no slavery the blacks might not be obese because sugar never would have become a staple without the "enslaved laborers who had no way to opt out of the treacherous work." [447]

Obesity is a lead contributing factor to hypertension and 40.3% of black adults have hypertension. Hypertension is greatly influenced by obesity, diabetes, and the use of salt. [448,449] The general diet of African Americans tends to include large amounts of salt.[450] For whites, Asians and Latinos hypertension ranged from 25% to 27.8%. Blacks have also been less likely than whites, Asians, or Latinos to engage in lifestyle changes and take their prescribed medicines to control hypertension. Someone with uncontrolled hypertension is three times more likely to die from a stroke, two times more likely to die from Covid-19, and four times more likely to die from a heart attack. [451,452,453,454]

People that are obese have increased risks for all-causes of death, type 2 diabetes, coronary heart disease, stroke, kidney disease, gallbladder disease, osteoarthritis, Alzheimer, sleep apnea and other breathing problems, amputations, difficulty functioning physically, mental illnesses, depression and many types of cancer. Obese people generally have a lower quality of life. Diabetes is the primary instigator of many diseases noted above. Most instances of diabetes are type II and eighty-nine percent of diabetics are overweight.[xl] Latinos, blacks, and Native Americans are disproportionately represented as diabetics. Latinos are 22% of the diabetic population, blacks 17%, and Native Americans 3.4%. For whites it was 51%, and Asians 5.6%.[455,xli] When it comes to different cancers people that are obese, and sometimes just overweight, have a 200% or more increased probability of developing endometrial cancer (women), esophageal adenocarcinoma, liver cancer, gastric cardia cancer, and kidney cancer. The increase is 10-50% for multiple

---

[xxxix] There was no breakout by race and gender, but women are 67% more likely to be severely obese than men.

[xl] Diabetes is present in 7.5% of whites, 9.2% of Asian Americans, 12.5% of Latinos, 11.7% of blacks, and 14.7% of Native Americans/Alaskan Natives.

[xli] Ethnic subgroups within Asians and Latinos show wide variations in diabetes, for example 5.6% of Chinese, and 12.6% of Indians. Among Latinos it is 6.5% of Cubans, 14.4% of Mexicans and 12.4% of Puerto Ricans.

myelomas, meningioma, pancreatic cancer, colorectal cancer: gallbladder cancer, breast cancer, and thyroid cancer.[456]

African American Dr. Richard White from the Mayo Clinic has studied the correlation between health literacy, chronic health diseases and obesity in minority populations. He said: "It's really going to require the African American community to come together as a unit to really say, 'you know what? This is our health as a community, this is something that we're going to take the initiative and interest to improve ourselves and not necessarily rely on outside or external forces to try and make it happen for us." [457] His advice appears to be spot on for the black community. In one study, it was found that African American health habits are not influenced by external sources, like medical doctors or government health advisories. Blacks, instead, must draw their own conclusions and then act on them.

Doctors and the healthcare system have also been unfairly cast as racist for failing to prescribe opioids to blacks for pain management. Articles, such as one from Project 1619, blame insufficient prescription pain medications to the perpetuation of racism from the period of slavery when doctors thought blacks had thicker skin and a greater tolerance for pain. It is true that up until 2010, blacks were not prescribed opioids as often. One reason for this is that blacks more than whites have been found to underreport the unpleasantness of pain in front of a doctor.[458] Another reason had to do with fewer blacks having prescription health care coverage. Monthly prescriptions for oxycontin, retail for over $200. Doctors have instead prescribed NSAIDs, like acetaminophen (i.e., Tylenol), or ibuprofen (i.e., Advil), which retail for under $10 for a monthly supply. Blacks are prescribed NSAIDs more than any racial group. Good news bad news, now that blacks have health insurance coverage equal to other racial groups blacks are equally likely to receive prescriptions for opioids, and there is now a "persistent reliance on opioids across all racial/ethnic groups." [459]

During the pandemic there was quite a bit of press given to the disproportionate outcomes for blacks and Latinos. The cry of racism and white privilege was loud even though it was known that people with pre-existing conditions had much higher risks. People that are obese were estimated to have a 300% greater risk of hospitalization. The ratio of hospitalizations to deaths has continually declined since the start of the pandemic, but it has ranged from 7% to 26%.The following pre-existing conditions posed the most risk of dying from Covid-19: cardiovascular disease (225% increase in risk), hypertension (182%), diabetes (148%), obesity (148%), congestive heart failure (203%), chronic kidney disease (325%), and cancer (147%).[460] As of January 2021, according to the CDC and the National Center for Health Statistics, the percentage of Covid deaths by race were 60.7% for whites, 15.6% for Latinos, 3.6% for Asians, 1.1% for Native Americans, and 16% for blacks.[461] The disproportionately high death rate for blacks must be viewed in conjunction with disproportionate health problems that influence Covid death rates. For example, blacks are 13.4% of the population, but they make up 19% of the obese population, 17% of diabetics, 40.3% of cases of hypertension, and 35% of people with kidney disease.[462,463,xlii] Disproportionate Covid outcomes look like an outcome of the disproportionate presence of many diseases that are greatly influenced by lifestyle choices, rather than racist doctors or a racist health care system.

[xlii] According to the Mayo Clinic, diabetes, obesity, hypertension, and cardiovascular disease are risk factors for kidney disease. A genetic link seems to be suggested by also listing African American as a risk factor, but the presence of kidney disease in sub-Saharan Africa ranges from 10.7% to 15.8%.

In a motion of equity or was it benevolent racism, priorities were given to vaccinating blacks and Latinos against Covid. Most Latinos have said they believe getting vaccinated is part of everyone's responsibility. [464] Most blacks said they didn't want the vaccine. Campaigns by black leaders to remember the Tuskegee Syphilis medical experiments of 1932 were rampant, and Louis Farrakhan promoted the theory that two white men, Anthony Fauci and Bill Gates created the vaccine to depopulate the earth. These types of comments are unhelpful to minimizing deaths from Covid.

There is a need for education on the history of medical experimentation in the United States and also in the world. People of all colors have participated in medical experiments, and before 1946 it was commonly without consent. Today, consent is required. In the United States 80-90% of all participants in medical experiments (clinical trials) are white, and participants do die and suffer adverse effects. They participate for the greater good, which can be motivated by looking for a personal cure. In 1993, Congress passed the National Institutes Health Revitalization Act which requires drug companies to diversity their subjects. Minorities and women have been heavily solicited. Women have signed up in numbers, but minorities rarely do. This is a real problem, especially for ailments that are more common to Asians, blacks or Latinos.[465] If minorities have disproportionate side effects to new medicines, this won't be due to racism, but rather a propensity of some racial/ethnic groups not to participate in clinical trials for new medical treatments.

It's hard to grasp the allegation that because blacks have higher hospitalization rates for influenza this is an indicator of racism in health care. Blacks have been 70% more likely than whites to be admitted to hospitals for influenza related reasons. For Latinos it was 15% higher. Asians were 13% less likely. The grandest contributor determining hospitalization was failing to get the flu vaccine. Vaccination rates have been significantly lower for blacks and Latinos. For the 2019-2020 flu season, 62% of Latinos were NOT vaccinated versus 59% of blacks, 48% of Asians and 47% of whites. Vaccination rates are especially important for older people and people that are obese. Vaccination has been proven to reduce flu-related hospitalizations for obese people by 79% and 40% for old people. High dose vaccines have been proven to reduce hospitalizations for old people by another 24%.[466,467,468] Between 70 and 85 percent of flu-related deaths are for people over 65. Older white people are the most likely to get vaccinated. Only 29% of old white people did NOT get vaccinated, and 44.5% of blacks, 47.4% of Asians, and 51.4% of Latinos did not.[469] Even people without health insurance can get vaccinated at no charge.[470] The reasons people don't get vaccinated are commonly personal. Latinos that don't get vaccinated offered a number of reasons including time, money, fear of needles, side effects, feeling healthy, and lack of information, interest or motivation. Whites commonly didn't get vaccinated because they didn't think getting the flu was a big deal. Blacks commonly didn't get vaccinated because of a history of racism. [471,472]

Differences in healthcare insurance by race do vary, and this may impact health outcomes, but this is not obvious. Medicaid has contributed to high rates of health insurance across races. Medicaid enrollees in 2019 were 34% black, 29% Latinos, 15% white, and 14% Asian. Today uninsured include 21% of Latinos, 11% of blacks, 11% of Asians, and 8% of whites. These are dramatic improvements from 2010, or pre the Affordable Care Act, where 32% of Latinos, 19.9% of blacks, 16.7% of Asians and 13.1% of whites were uninsured. It might seem like increasing access to health care would improve health outcomes, but this has not been evident, with the exception of a decrease in mental health problems for Latinos.[473,474, 475,476,477,478, xliii,xliv,xlv]

The Affordable Care Act is one of the earlier implementations of equitable programs. It is a good program to show how cost sharing changes with equitable solutions. While participants in Medicaid have no-to-low cash outlay for medical services, the cost of these services has increased and significantly for those with no insurance or private insurance.[479,480]

Ninety-four percent of doctors are non-black. This too has been pointed to as a product of racism, but 17% of doctors are Asian.[481] Medical schools, like universities all over America have been making concerted efforts to diversify by encouraging blacks and Latinos to apply and also by offering scholarships. A grand challenge for blacks and Latinos is that the pool of potential applicants is lower for a number of reasons. The high school dropout rate for Latinos is 8.6%. For blacks it is 6.1%, whites 5.2% and Asians 3%. In 2019 just 51% of black high school graduates enrolled in college vs 63% of Latinos, 67% of whites, and 90% of Asians. [482,483, 484] Some have pointed at racism as the reason for lower enrollments, but this is nonsense. Discrimination doesn't affect college enrollment, unless you count positive discrimination. Universities have diversity missions that specifically seek black and Latino students. Many schools' lower qualifications for SAT and ACT scores, and GPAs. Positive discrimination also impacts financial assistance. Blacks were most likely to receive financial aid to attend college (88%). For Latinos it was 82%. [485]

Positive discrimination helps with college enrollment but to get into med school, all students must graduate, and they must have reasonably good MCAT scores and grades. The requirement for a bachelor's degree or higher cuts the possible pool down to 15% of Latinos, 21% of blacks, 35% of whites, and 54% of Asians. [486] Then people must apply. In 2020, applications by race to med school were 8% black, 10% Latino, 23% Asian, and 43% white.[487] Acceptance rates were lower for blacks. It was 38% for blacks vs. 43% for Latinos, 44% for Asians, and 45% for whites. [488, 489] Racism? The two primary criteria to determine admissions into medical school are MCAT scores and GPAs. Schools that have the lowest acceptance rate on MCATs hover in the low 500s, although two schools accept MCATs at 498 and 499. Acceptable GPAs are rarely below 3.5. Average MCAT scores for black applicants were 497.6 and 499.9 for Native Americans. All other races had average scores above 500. (The highest possible score is 528.) The average GPA for black applicants was 3.33. For Native Americans it was 3.41, Latinos 3.44, Asians 3.63, and whites 3.64. [490] A disproportionate presence of medical doctors by race is not due to racism.

Disparate outcomes in health care are more likely for women than for people of different races/ethnicities. This is because biological differences between men and women are significant. This is much less so by race. [491,492] It is possible that there could be improved health outcomes for different ethnicities with greater participation in medical

---

^{xliii} The absence of healthcare does not preclude access to healthcare. Thirty-six states have facilities that provide free or low-cost healthcare to people with limited income. Also, emergency health care cannot be denied to anyone for any reason.

^{xliv} The largest population of uninsured are young people (19-34) that do not qualify for Medicaid and choose not to purchase health care because they don't see the need.

^{xlv} Latinos, the largest uninsured population does have a life expectancy of 81.9 years, which is longer than all groups but Asian Americans (86.3).

trials, and also with physician diversity. The latter appears to be most important to the black community because there is no evidence of other racial groups expressing skepticism of doctors from another race or ethnicity.[xlvi] Because of this, it is probably better to say that more black doctors could help to improve health outcomes for the black community. This has nothing to do with racist doctors and everything to do with black patients being more comfortable and trusting of black doctors that have greater familiarity with black culture. Greater physician diversity, beyond more Asian diversity, is not, however, going to occur until Latinos and blacks improve their educational performance. A more immediate path for better health outcomes for all people is possible by taking the advice of Dr. White to take the initiative and interest to improve healthy habits. For some, that requires an end to blaming racism for poor health outcomes and accepting personal responsibility.

[xlvi] During the pandemic there were anecdotes of eastern Asian doctors and nurses facing discrimination. This was tied to an increase in discrimination for eastern Asians due to the presumed Chinese origins of the virus.

Living up to a commitment to equality of opportunity

America's history offers so many reasons for Americans to be proud of their country. In the history of the world, America is unique in many ways. It was the first colony of any empire to revolt and win their independence. The was from the British Empire! As a new nation in 1776, she stunned the world by creating a foundation where government was by the people and for the people and where the factors of production would be owned by people rather than the state. The foundation was a democratic government and a capitalist economic system. It was a foundation that could be built upon to enable every American the chance to be successful beyond what was possible in the nations where they or their ancestors came from. Originally, the most likely to succeed were Protestant white men. Most blacks were enslaved. The limited rights of women left them in virtual slavery, and the Irish and Jews could find signs telling them they need not apply. Some joked that they didn't need signs for the Italians because they couldn't read. Jokes aside, there were opportunities for anyone willing to work hard and smart. This was the beauty of a foundation of democracy and capitalism. There was nothing like it in the world.

Some had the luck of being beneficiaries in the wills of people that had worked hard and acquired wealth. Thousands of free blacks inherited land and other assets from their former white employers. Some were former slave masters and fathers. A couple dozen black women inherited an enormous amount of wealth from their white male partners. They couldn't marry, but that didn't mean they couldn't be in love and live together. Black and mulatto beneficiaries leveraged hard work to increase the value of their inheritance and they were respected by blacks and whites for being hard workers and enterprising. In 1860, there were 1,391 wealthy black families in the south. In 1870 the number rose to 3,092.[493,xlvii]

In the north in the mid-1800s, Jeremiah Hamilton became America's first black millionaire. He was nicknamed the Prince of Darkness. Many that worked with him were said to be uninterested in the color of his skin. It was the color of his money. [494] It was at a similar time when Hetty Green, the Witch of Wall Street, became the wealthiest woman in America. Hetty made a fortune, but she also came from wealth. Mary Ellen Pleasant became the first self-made female African American millionaire in the mid 1800s. Her fortune today would be measured with nine zeroes. [495]

Joseph Banigan and his family escaped the Irish potato famine by coming to America in 1847. Clever and hardworking, in the latter part of the 19th century, he became one of America's first (or the first) Irish Catholic millionaire. In this time, Catholics, Jews and atheists were denied some rights, even though it was barred by the US constitution. They were not, however denied the right to become educated. The Irish, in general, saw in America opportunities they could never have imagined in Great Britain. The same was true for Jews arriving from Europe. Both ethnoreligious groups highly valued and leveraged education. By 1900, the average income for Irish people was the same as the average for the nation. By 1900, Jews were disproportionately holding positions of economic power. Less than 0.1% of the population, Jews held 3.4% of top corporate positions.[496]

Initially, the Italians didn't see success being tied to education. They weighted building work skills over education. This was the path to making a living in Italy. They soon

---

[xlvii] A person that was wealthy had at least $2,000 in land. Two thousand dollars in crop land in 1860 is worth about $2 million today.

realized that in America they could make more than a living, but they had to embrace the value of education. Having a son in college became the ticket for being recognized as an up and comer. One of the earliest Italian American success stories was Amadeo Gianni. He created the Bank of Italy in San Francisco in 1904. Uniquely, it was a bank for everyman. In 1928 he merged his bank to form Bank of America.

In the early 1900s, the fruits of America's foundation were working for the nation. While the south had been engaged in agriculture, the north was in the midst of an industrial revolution. The United States soon became the largest manufacturer in the world. There was some manufacturing in the south. This included African American Andrew Dunford, a manufacturer of cotton gins.

The little American upstart dismissed around the world for its innovations in political and economic systems was now financier to giant empires in WWI. America had shunned imperialism and mostly limited its business dealings to North America. She was a reluctant participant in WWI. President Woodrow Wilson only agreed to America becoming an Allied Power on the condition that people in the losing empires would be given their freedom, rather than handed over for subjugation to yet another empire. The grandest beneficiary of this stipulation was Arab Muslims in the Middle East. One thing was for sure: a neophyte calling for people to be free was unpopular in the early 1900s.

America became essential again to victory in WWII and to the world not being overrun by dictatorial fascists that believed the world needed to physically eliminate people that were different. The fascists found some people deplorable, including Chinese, Jews, Slavic, Roma (gypsies), and blacks. Franklin Delano Roosevelt parlayed military victory in WWII to ensure that Africans and Asians would be free from colonial subordination, and to get commitments from all nations to end discrimination by ensuring fundamental freedoms for all. In addition to this, after 2,000 years of persecution, Jewish people all over the world would have a country to live in where their freedoms would be protected. Having this much power to do this much good was a testament to the power of a democratic capitalist foundation fueling a diverse population integrated by the American Creed.

As one of two superpowers during the Cold War, America took the lead in trying to ensure that Americans and the world would not have to trade freedom-loving democracy and wealth producing capitalism for a socialist system that had murdered tens of millions for the crime of disagreeing with a freedomless existence that ensured equal impoverishment and repression for all. The exceptional role that America has played in making the world a freer place, in promoting equal fundamental freedoms for all, and for building a foundation that permits anyone to achieve a better life is admired throughout the world. Equally admired is the unparalleled progress it has made in building an equal opportunity multiracial state. Most nations ignored post-WWII commitments to end discrimination, but America became an anti-racist role model. America's Declaration of Independence (1776) said, "we hold these truths to be self-evident that all men are created equal." What did that mean in 1776? After WWII, it came to mean exactly what it said, and America became the world's anti-racist leader.

One key to America's prosperity has been a belief in social mobility. Most nations have relatively fixed social hierarchies. People are born and die in the same social level. Fixed hierarchies deliver order. From one generation to the next, the same people are rich or poor, rulers or subordinates. America is different. It has a flexible hierarchy. Contrary to a common misconception, the "upper class" is rarely a product of inheritance, and most Americans (56%) will be a member of the top 10% club at some point in their lives. Most Americans start out in the bottom 20%, 95% exit, and 56% make it to the top 10%.[497] These are the outcomes of people of every color and creed seeking out opportunity and running with it. In America, individual achievement drives wealth. Not birthrights, inheritance, color, or religion.

In America, success is up to you. America's government and economic foundation allow aspirational anyones to exceed the success of their parents and even their wildest dreams. People have the chance to rise to the top or plunge to the bottom, and they do it all the time. This flexible hierarchy is a recipe for social disorder rather than order. This disorder is the price Americans pay for a social mobility that never pigeonholes someone into a miserable impoverished existence. That outcome is reserved for the masses in socialist and other autocratic systems.[xlviii] This disorder has allowed a family of four that is completely supported by social welfare to have, on average, more money than families with a working parent in 90% of the countries of the world.

The United States is unique in producing thousands of rags-to-riches stories, and almost as many riches-to-rags stories. Early on most stories, but definitely not all, were for male, Protestants, of northern European blood. After 1945, and then again after 1964 (Civil Rights Act) America's numerous commitments to anti-racism and anti-sexism have opened up opportunities for men and women of diverse ethnicities and religions. Now diverse groups are scaling and descending America's flexible social hierarchy. In 2020, 23% of America's millionaires were people of color, split pretty evenly among Asians, blacks and Latinos.[498] Specific numbers for women are less clear because most are married, and their assets are pooled with their spouses. In 2020, there were, however, 21 self-made American female billionaires, and 100 women with self-made fortunes exceeding $150 million.[499] They are Asian, black, white, Latina, cisgender and LGBTQ. This could only happen in America!

Equality of opportunity, equality, and equity. Some people think America's commitment to equality of opportunity and treating people equally before the law, translates into social equality or equity. Some version of "from each according to his ability, to each according to his needs." That's socialism. The stuff of Stalin, Lenin, Marx, Mao, Bernie Sanders, CRT, Alexandra Ocasio-Cortez, and Patrisse Cullors. In the end, the quote more often cited in socialist spheres is, "they pretend to pay us, and we pretend to work." When the Berlin Wall came down in 1989, the world was finally able to see how economies and societies crumble when people pretend to work. Fans of socialism, like Sanders, CRT advocates, Ocasio-Cortez, and Cullors could, however, cheer because one goal of socialism is to eliminate millionaires and billionaires, and this was achieved -- except among political elites.

America offers equality of opportunity. Every American has the chance to avail themselves to opportunities. This has been and remains the single biggest driver of most Americans rising from the bottom 20% to the top 10% and the greatest inducement for people to immigrate to America. In most of the world, people do not have equality of opportunity, and they may not even have access to anything that could reasonably be called an opportunity. Equality of opportunity has been the driver of America's extraordinary

---

[xlviii] Citizens in autocratic oil states in the Middle East and Brunei Darussalam often have high qualities of life.

prosperity. This prosperity allows Americans to transfer an amount of wealth for social welfare that exceeds the GDPs of 177/193 nations. It is a prosperity that has fueled the rise of America to become a political, military and economic superpower. This has set the stage for a nation of people unafraid of challenges, unafraid of naysayers, unafraid of what people are thinking, unafraid of success. A nation of people that know if they want to succeed, they simply have to avail themselves to opportunities.

Social Democrats and other CRT advocates have called America's mixed-capitalist economic system slavery 2.0 and racist because financial outcomes are disproportional by race. (Re-invoking slavery is really powerful theatre.) Unequal financial outcomes have everything to do with economics and nothing to do with race. People that produce more are paid more. If someone wants to be paid more, all they have to do is produce more. Socialism is more akin to slavery 2.0. If someone wants to be paid more there is no option. Aspiring for a better life is like wishing on a star. [500, 501]

Many non-black Americans saw the election of Barack Obama as proof positive that the final chapter on racism had been written. Many around the world agreed. Only a non-racist white nation would elect a black man to be president, and only a non-racist nation would have an army of globally prominent African Americans in all facets of life: Hollywood, business, medicine, academia, government, and sports.

Some argued that having the most educated and prosperous black community in the world was a distraction from the issue that all black people did not have equal opportunities because they faced discrimination. This was plainly evident in black household income being about 40% lower than whites. Was it plainly evident? Blacks have far more single-parent households. Different studies show this negatively affects household income by 11-62%, with an average of 32%.[502] According to US Census data from 2020, 11% of white households were single parent and 64% of black households were single parent. Most blacks also live in the states with the lowest pay scales – the south. Per capita incomes in most southern states are about 40% less than the average for the country. Combine per capita income differences by location with a high percentage of single parent households and a significant portion of the difference in household income is explained. Still, people have dug in on racism as the reason blacks have fewer opportunities.

They can dig all they like. There is plenty of other data that shows America is a land of equal opportunity for those that seek it. At birth everyone in America does have equality of opportunity. Where it goes from there is determined by parents and individuals. Do people seek to improve their educational outcomes, build skill levels, and relocate to be near better opportunities? Do they prepare themselves to compete with other candidates?

Parents make a big difference by getting and staying married. The poverty rate for children in two parent families of any race or ethnicity is 7.5%. In 2019, the poverty rate for single parent households that were black was 27.3%, whites 17.1%, and Latinos 26.8%. Want to take a torch to poverty? Encourage people of all races to get and stay married and teach children the importance of education. [503,504]

Another factor that influences opportunities is, who you know. Where someone lives, goes to school, and spends free time affects who they know. This is where decisions to live in communities of like people or self-segregation, hurt blacks and Latinos. Integrated communities offer far more opportunities. This is because the white and Asian racial groups have achieved greater success and there is no shortage of either that takes a special interest in helping young people of any color or creed that really want to succeed.

Where one chooses to live can affect access to opportunities for another reason. The best opportunities don't grow on nearby trees; they congregate in different locations. And different locations offer different professional opportunities. For example, Silicon Valley, Austin, or Boston for technology. Choosing where one lives also affects quality of life that can affect motivations. In some communities, for example, crime can be higher, and infrastructure, including those that deliver clean water, can be of poor-quality.

When the Civil Rights Act of 1964 was enacted, blacks were 10.5% of the population, Latinos were 3%, Asians 0.5%, and mixed race 0%. America's newer immigration policy dramatically diversified the nation. A nation that was 86% white in 1964, in 2020 was 60% non-Hispanic white, 18.5% Latino, 13.4% black, 5.7% Asian, 1.2% Native American/Alaskan and Hawaiian.[xlix] When it came to the workforce, there was another huge change. The participation rate of women had doubled between 1964 and 2019. It had gone from 38.3% to 76.8%. In the 1960s blacks filled diversity targets, now 70% of the population is competing to fill these targets. Indeed, this highly diverse population is competing to fill all opportunities with or without targets. Education, experience, and a desire to achieve all matter.

Everyone in America begins life with equality of opportunity. From there it's up to parents and individuals. In 2005, a leading thinker on race in America, African American Shelby Steele said: "I absolutely, 100 percent believe that if you want to do something in American society, whatever it may be--I'm not saying you will not encounter any racism, but racism will not stop you."[505] Sounds like equality of opportunity. And that was fifteen years ago! If someone wants equity or social equality, they might want to try immigrating to Cuba or Venezuela. That's what their systems promise and deliver. Everyone is equally poor, and they have no opportunities – so its equal.

[xlix] Mixed race in 1960 wasn't counted. Today, mixed race populations are understated because the United States is unusual in traditionally counting and seeing mulattoes as black, and because many mixed-raced Latinos identify as white. The latter is a common practice in Latam.

Integration and multiculturalism

In Europe, Russia, and China the solution to warring adjacent ethnicities was to create a common nationality and then encourage integration or assimilation. This was a formula for creating homogeneity from diversity and enabling multi-ethnic or -racial states to peacefully coexist and prosper. Europe is generally credited with the original idea of developing homogeneity from diversity.[1] It was motivated by a need to stop endless wars between diverse ethnicities. China was last to realize the importance of people sharing the common bonds of nationality. Ethnic conflict including the Taiping Rebellion (1850-1864) where 20-30 million died, and a Century of Humiliation inflicted by powers with common nationalities, convinced China to change. In the 20th century China forced, rather than encouraged, people to assimilate into a Han Chinese culture so there would be a common language, values and culture.

In the early 20th century, the nations of Czechoslovakia and Yugoslavia were created from diverse ethnic and religious groups. The arrival of communism after WWII thwarted efforts to create a common nationality. Everyone was a comrade, right? After communism ended in the late 20th century, both nations imploded. In Yugoslavia, it was explosive, and the outcome was seven nations. If only they had developed a common nationality.

Beginning in the mid-20th century, Europe began adding diversity to its homogenous white, Christian populations. Many European nations chose to segregate the new populations and practice multiculturalism. Multiculturalism allows different populations to live in separate communities where they are given the freedom to maintain their cultures. It's an implementation of separate but equal. In other European nations people were free to integrate, but many populations chose to self-segregate, implementing self-multiculturalism. In the early 21st century when fascist (ultra-nationalistic) political parties were gaining popularity in many European countries, multiculturalism that was encouraged or self-decided was pronounced a failure. It was realized that there was no separate but equal. Encouraging integration into a common nationality, like that which was common in the United States, was recognized as the only way to peacefully govern a multi-ethnic -racial state.

For two hundred years, immigrants to the United States knew if they wanted to experience equality of opportunity unmarred by discrimination, they had to become Americans. The Americanization process is gradual, and it is not forced. It relies on immigrants wanting to integrate or assimilate. For the Italians and Irish, this took multiple generations, and it was filled with angst and feelings of displacement from abandoning ethnic traditions. Ironically, assimilating or integrating into America does not call for abandoning ethnic traditions and celebrations.[506] Still, perceptions can overtake reality. What it does require is adopting the American Creed. Today that includes speaking English, a hard work ethic, individualism (being self-reliant),[li] being educated, and a belief in the rule of law. Most immigrants to America came from nations where repression was stifling, with no possibility to exit poverty, limited access to education and scant opportunities to realize dreams. They adopted the American Creed because they knew it

---

[1] Some International Relations' writers attribute the origin of the nation-state to the Peace of Westphalia (1648), while others vigorously contest this. Notwithstanding the disagreement, there is agreement that nation-states have homogenous populations, and homogeneity has to be developed.

[li] Individualism is a belief in being self-reliant. This is in contrast to a reliance on the state.

was key to ending discrimination that impedes access to opportunities. Every different population in America has faced discrimination until they have adopted the basic values in the Creed.

Ethnic, racial, or religious populations that shun basic national values routinely face conscious or unconscious discrimination all over the world. It's a human response for people to discriminate against people that espouse different values. In many countries, integration requires quite a bit more than adopting basic national values, and in some nations, there are strict cultural requirements, and the process of integrating is not gradual or voluntary. In some nations, ethnic groups won't integrate or assimilate because the requirements are too onerous, for example, some will not give up or they cannot give up their religion. Muslims in India might find less discrimination, which can be intense and legal, if they converted to Hinduism, but Islam prohibits this.[507,508] China's assimilation process, Sinicization, requires political and cultural conformity. The latter includes religious conformity. Everyone sings from the same hymnal. It also includes thought conformity. The Communist Party has strict controls on speech, and it invests in controlling people's thoughts. This is not something akin to ineffective unconscious bias training. Chinese that diverge from the Party line, as in the Communist Party line, will undergo re-education, which has been compared to brainwashing. Re-education "camps are forced ideological and behavioral reeducation centers, run in secret to rewire inmates' thinking." There are more than a 1,000 camps and millions of Chinese have been re-educated in these camps. [509,510]

To integrate in America, one did have to be free. For most blacks, integration was impossible until 1865. Even afterwards, many chose to self-segregate. In the 1940s, 1950s, 1960s, and 1970s programs, laws, and policies were put in place to facilitate the integration of blacks and Native Americans. Progress was constant. Then in the 1960s, American politicians started rethinking the successful melting pot formula. A focus on integrating Native Americans, which was partially successful, was altered. Legislation was passed in the 1960s and 1970s to provide additional government funded services to facilitate education and health care on Native American reservations. It was a separate but equal formula. It hasn't worked out so well. The 22% of Native Americans that live on reservations experience greater hardships than most that have chosen to enter mainstream America. Those that have integrated into the mainstream of urban and suburban areas also express fewer perceptions of discrimination.

Separate but equal hasn't worked out well for blacks either. Millions of black people in multiple migrations between 1910 and 1970 moved to other parts of the country that offered more and better opportunities. When the War on Poverty programs commenced, blacks lost much of their motivation to move for better opportunities that could land them in integrated communities. Blacks that chose self-segregation might not have access to the best opportunities or the best living environments, but they were not so discontent to move and integrate with whites. That is their right. America is a free country. Groups can self-segregate to live in multicultural communities. This decision places a priority on preserving ethnic/racial/cultural differences and consciously or unconsciously decrements the priority on economic outcomes. The cities with the highest segregation of blacks and whites have the greatest rates of black poverty. Latinos that self-segregate also experience diminished economic outcomes.[511,lii] So do Native Americans. According to the US

[lii] Segregated Cuban communities did not have higher poverty.

Census, depending on the reservation, poverty can be twice as high as for Native Americans overall.[liii] Multiculturalism and self-segregation are anti-formulas for building multiracial states that offer equality of opportunity, but America is a free country. If people don't want to avail themselves to opportunities, that is their right.[liv]

Many blacks striving for a better life continue to migrate and often to the suburbs, but also to cities in the West and Midwest. This is where the best integration outcomes have been found for blacks and whites, and the best economic opportunities for blacks. In all of these states, the black population is less than 7%. The best economic mobility for blacks is in the north and west, but blacks tend to live in regions and cities where upward mobility is relatively low. A person cannot avail themselves to better opportunities when they do not exist where they live. [512,513,514, 515]

In the 1990s a chorus of people began talking about integration as unkind. Even the basic requirement for people to speak English was being questioned. Some schools began teaching in Spanish and some taught Ebonics, now called the African American Vernacular English (AAVE). Both fell under ridicule. The Spanish language survived for a while but AAVE did not, but now it is making a comeback. People arguing that a focus on standard English would lessen a basis for unconscious bias and improve opportunities have been pilloried as racists. Some argued that countries all over the world have multiple dialects, and schools don't teach in dialects, so why would America? It was argued that teaching in a dialect is unnecessary because it is simple for children to pick up other languages through repetition at school. It is also harmful, because it inhibits learning. How many books, textbooks, magazines, and papers are written in AAVE? How much vocal media is in AAVE? Schools have mostly abandoned teaching in Spanish. Schools and parents alike recognize that there is no equality of opportunity for people that do not speak standard English. But AAVE is gaining in receptivity. Some schools are now looking at teaching students and teachers how to code switch between AAVE and standard English.

Many argue that integration is hard, but it is hardly unkind. There are countless articles that discuss the richness and numerous benefits of diversity, for example, expanding access to opportunities and learning from diverse points of view. Georgetown University law professor, Sheryll Cashin, has written on the failures of blacks and whites to integrate. She notes that 85% of whites are indifferent to the skin color of their neighbors. (In 2013, the World Values Survey placed it at over 95%.[516]) This contrasts with Michelle Obama's memoir where she said: "I want to remind white folks that y'all were running from us and you're still running." [517] Turns out blacks and whites run from neighborhoods for the same reason. They care about crime, the quality of schools their children attend, public services, and stable property values. Black flight occurs for the same reasons as white flight. This has led both middle-class blacks and whites to live as neighbors. Blacks and whites with similar goals, values, and income levels integrate well, just like Americans of other races and ethnicities.

Cashin notes that "even at the height of the civil rights era, socializing with whites was never a goal in itself for black people, and undoubtedly for many, it is not one today." [518]

[liii] On 8 out of 10 of the largest reservations, the percentage living in poverty was 41-59%. Rates of poverty in predominantly black or Latino communities can be similarly high.
[liv] Segregated black communities are most common in the south, where, per the 2010 Census, 54% of blacks live. It was 90% in 1900.

Before the civil rights era, it wasn't applauded either. African American author Zora Neale Hurston (1891-1960) rejected integration with whites. In 1968 the Hyde County Boycotts protested against sending their children to integrated schools. Blacks not wanting to integrate with whites after the history of slavery and later Jim Crow might have seemed reasonable, but people like Martin Luther King knew that integration was key to so much that ailed racial relations and important to progress for blacks in America. "People fail to get along because they fear each other; they fear each other because they don't know each other; they don't know each other because they have not communicated with each other." Integration is the antidote to this fear.

The pace of integration between blacks and whites has stagnated, but this is less a function of any discrimination and more a preference that minority populations have for living with like people. There is considerable research that shows the positive effects on income, education, and crime when moving to neighborhoods with low poverty, which commonly means more whites and Asians. But many don't care to live in these neighborhoods. The US government has invested in many programs to encourage low-income African Americans and Latinos to move to integrated neighborhoods that offer superior opportunities. What they have found is that people instead move to like neighborhoods, and in some cases use vouchers to return to their old neighborhoods. When people have chosen this path, positive improvements in education for their children or family income did not materialize.[519,520] One outcome from these programs should be that whites and the government recognize that for blacks and Latinos the comfort of like people can be more important than increasing their incomes and opportunities and improving their living environments.

A preference for self-segregation by blacks, Latinos or Native Americans is understandable from the perspective that it may reduce perceptions of discrimination in their communities that can make life seem more comfortable. However, it does not create safer communities, improve educational outcomes or create a foundation for better economic opportunities. To the contrary, minority neighborhoods generally have higher crime, quality of education is lower and dropout rates are higher in high school and college. [521,522,523,524] Many cite the challenges for poorer people to move, although the continuous arrival of millions of poorer immigrants to America indicates that desires for better opportunities can lead to accepting and surmounting challenges. Still, government programs have shown that given the means, low-income blacks and Latinos were inclined to choose the comfort of segregated communities over the chance for better schools, environments and economic opportunities. Leaving the comfort of living with like people is part of the integration process that leads to equality of opportunity. But in America, integration is not forced. If people prioritize comfort over opportunities, that is their right.

The growing expenditures on government assistance and cultures of victimization have been unhelpful to encouraging integration and so are the missives of black academicians on an ostensible mission of stirring up trouble between blacks and whites. Kendi has accused whites of "lynching black culture." Kendi loves to pepper his writing with the word lynch when making references to white people. But the question for Kendi is, how does the identity of an American as English speaking, self-reliant, embracing a hard work ethic, educated, and accepting the inherent equality of rule of law, lynch blacks or anyone of their culture? I think I know the answer. Some see the American Creed as racist. Go to the African American Museum of History, and you can see for yourself. There you will find an area on White Culture. Not American Culture—White Culture. White Culture -- acting white -- includes self-reliance, individualism, hard work, standard English, and the rule of law. It also includes the nuclear family and the scientific method, including objective rational thinking. [lv] These are qualities of so-called acting white. This has come to mean being at odds with black culture.

Another question for Kendi is, if not integration with whites, then what? Self-segregation, self-imposed multiculturalism? Every implementation of multiculturalism from South African apartheid, to Europe's isolation of migrant workers, and the use of "reservations" or "nations" for New World indigenous populations has failed. In multiracial societies, there is no separate but equal.

Integration stands alone as the one proven way multiracial nations can successfully build national identities that end perceptions of discrimination and deliver equality of opportunity. Irish Americans and Italian Americans are a testament to the power of integration. More recently Asian Americans and Latino Americans have been undergoing or progressing integration with good outcomes. [525,lvi] This has been taking place even with perceived levels of discrimination for Asians and Latinos that was similar to blacks.[526] Asian Americans count among the most recent immigrant group to reap the benefits of integration. According to the IMF, per capita income in India in 2020 was $1,877. For Indian Americans it was $120,000. Latinos are reaping benefits too. The qualities of life Latinos have in America are continually improving and far exceed the lives from where they came. Per capita income in Mexico in 2020 was $8,069. In Honduras, Guatemala, and El Salvador it was $2,421, $3,821 and $4,240 respectively. Household income for American Latinos averages just over $60,000.

There are also data for improved outcomes for blacks that integrate, for example, superior economic outcomes in the west where blacks and whites have improved integration outcomes. Superior economic outcomes for blacks in states where black populations are less concentrated.[527] There are also supportive data related to the immigration of black immigrants (vs. US origin blacks). Black immigrants are much more likely to live in the west or the north where economic mobility is higher and there are fewer concentrated black communities. Relative to US origin blacks, black immigrants have household incomes that are on average 31% higher. They are 37% more likely to have a college degree, and 39% more likely to be married. They are also less likely to hold deep seated biases against whites. Nigerian Americans had a median household income in 2018 of $68,658. In Nigeria the per capita income is $2,149. (Nigeria has the 7th highest per capita income of the 46 countries in sub-Saharan Africa.) The number of black immigrants to America has been skyrocketing from black majority nations in sub-Saharan Africa and the Caribbean. In 2018 there were 4.8 million foreign-born blacks in the United States.[528,lvii] It can easily be that America to these black immigrants is a land where blacks can dream big, like being president, CEO, or the richest woman in the world. Dreams they

---

[lv] In July of 2020, the Smithsonian apologized for featuring the "White Culture" chart. Presumably it had been featured since 2003. The chart was created by diversity/unconscious bias consultant Judith Katz in 1990.

[lvi] Most Asian Americans strongly identify with the United States. They also identify with the cultures of their descendants. This is also true of many Latinos. To some degree it is true of multigenerational hyphenated white Americans and Canadians, but it has diminished over time. This is an outcome of assimilation. Dr. Peter Skerry of Boston College presents assimilation as having economic, social, cultural and political components. Most often the component immigrants hold onto is cultural.

[lvii] Immigrants from sub-Saharan Africa have increased 300% since 2000, and 1500% since 1980. There has been a similar increase for blacks from the Caribbean.

could not have had back home.[529] They can see America as an accessible land of opportunity. If they encounter racism or perceive biased thoughts, they may find it less than what they are used to back home, and not a deterrent to achieving what are likely impossible dreams back home. The story of these African immigrants has the familiar sound of so many immigrant groups that preceded them. Be self-reliant, independent, become educated, speak English, observe the rule of law, and become available for opportunities, and they will come. Perceptions of discrimination will naturally fade. This is America, the most successful multiracial nation in the world.

Conclusion

America is being held captive by poverty pimps and race hustlers. They have managed to secure a huge following of misguided social justice advocates and political opportunists. Together they have been perpetuating a false narrative of white oppression, black victimhood, systemically racist America, white supremacy, and white privilege. Lacking data, they recall events, many apocryphal, that can date to 1619, 1776, 1865, 1950 or 1962 and pretend these events happened yesterday. To support the narratives, they call on the Racists Law of Disproportionality. If disproportional than racist. Everyday there are stories blaming disproportionate outcomes in the criminal justice, education, and health care systems on racism. Racism is the new number 42 – the answer to everything. In reality, it has become a reflexive erroneous diagnosis for every area of life where minorities have performed worse than whites.

There is, however, another problem with 42. Asians are on average more prosperous and educated than whites. So are Jews and Nigerian Americans. Latino prosperity and education have surpassed blacks. That kills systemic racism, white oppression, white supremacy, and white privilege. Because of this the narrative has morphed. It is systemic racism, but just against black people. This narrative is problematic too. African Americans are the most prosperous and educated black population in the world. They also account for nearly every famous black person known around the world. The extraordinary success of so many African Americans is a problem in itself for the claims of racism against blacks because racist societies dislike all members of a particular group.

In America's discrimination circus, so much time is wasted on the racist bogeyman, there is no time to tackle the biggest impediment that prevents so many Americans from expanding access to opportunities. This is improving educational outcomes. The teachers' unions have co-opted too many elected officials and influential black leaders to voice support for the impossible task of "fixing public schools" as the only option. Fixing the public school system is about as likely as building an escalator to the moon. The public education system has been broken for half a century. It's a giant bureaucratic dinosaur that is stymied by unions that are doing their job of securing more for their members at the expense of a nation, with a disproportionate impact on blacks and Latinos.

Charter schools are key. Every child regardless of means must have access to an education that can prepare them to have a comfortable life. The support of billionaire white families has really helped, but more is needed. Every child with a good education is a child poised to succeed in life. Superior educational outcomes are also associated with a propensity to dismiss negative stereotypes, have a higher receptivity to racial integration, and a belief in egalitarianism.[530] Because a good education, by definition, cannot handicap a child, that means Project 1619 has no place in school, but endeavors like Project 1776 that celebrate black achievement and reject black victimhood are great options to expand American history courses. This would allow all Americans to again celebrate American heroes like George Washington, Abraham Lincoln, and Ulysses S. Grant, along with Frederick Douglas, W.E.B. Du Bois, and Martin Luther King.

A good education won't happen without a home and community life that supports education. It would be ideal if parents of all races really weighed the importance to children and the nation of raising their children together. It is not an American badge of honor that we have the highest percentage of single-parent households in the world.

With or without both parents at home, there is a need for multiracial tiger moms and dads, and we need communities of all colors supporting children's efforts to become educated. An aversion to acting white cannot pertain to education, self-reliance, hard work, speaking English, and rule of law. Perhaps blacks beholden to not acting white can hold their noses when they act white (or act Asian or Latino) in these areas, knowing it will improve their economic outcomes, lessen reliance on Slavery 2.0, reduce perceptions of discrimination, and improve health outcomes.

People with higher levels of education, generally, have healthier lifestyles and live longer. The United States ranks 36th among nations for longevity, which is horrible. Some racial/ethnic groups fare worse than others. The gap between Asians, the racial group with the highest educational outcomes, and blacks, the racial group with the lowest education outcomes is a whopping nine years. America's poor longevity ranking ties closely to something else that is not an American badge of honor; an obesity epidemic that has been accompanied by an epidemic of sedentary lifestyles. Studies have shown that just one additional year of education can reduce the prevalence of obesity by 4-8%.[531] Imagine the benefits less obesity could have on the presence of some diseases and illnesses, and the costs of health care.

The urgency to fix education in America is needed for so many reasons, and one reason of extraordinary importance is the relationship between diminished educational outcomes and crime. Instead of fixing education, government leaders and social justice advocates are pushing to defund the police and legalize crime for some populations. It's so much easier to pass laws that undermine a pillar of America's foundation – the rule of law -- than to fix education. Rule of law is essential to protecting America's free society along with public safety. It is being sacrificed by self-righteous people calling for twisted ideas of social justice and equity because they can't or won't address the real underlying problems.

Next time you hear someone say systemically racist America, ask if the source is the original sin of slavery, the original sin of racism, the fugitive slave clause, or unconsciously biased thoughts. If you hear white privilege, ask if it relates to flesh tone band-aids, or the inability to buy music by black or Latino artists. Knowledge is power and Americans cannot be silenced every time someone whips out the R, S, or P words.

While the pimps and hustlers endeavor to keep millions stuck in victimhood or on the hook suffering white guilt, this opens up even more opportunities for those that know America is the land of opportunity for people of every color and creed. It's important to seize these opportunities so American greatness won't be sacrificed to the greatest con job the world has ever seen.

Bibliography

1 Douglass, Frederick, What the Black Man Wants. Utc.iath.virginai.edu, retrieved January 7, 2021.

2 Walter Williams: Suffer No Fools - Full Video, Free to Choose Network. December 29, 2015.

3 Elder, Larry. The secret story of blacks' success. Baltimore Sun, September 8, 2004.

4 Falk, Gene. Low-Income Assistance Programs: Trends in Federal Spending. Congressional Research Service, May 4, 2014.

5 The Population of Poverty USA. PovertyUSA.org, retrieved February 7, 2021.

6 Poverty in the United States: 2000, Census.gov, September 2001.

7 US Census data for different years.

8 Rector, Robert, Menon, Vijay. Understanding the Hidden $1.1 Trillion Welfare System and How to Reform It. Heritage.org, August 5, 2018.

9 24 Welfare Statistics & Facts. Balancing Everything. February 16, 2021.

10 Are these the end days of the extortionist era of Civil Rights. Issues and Views – The Blog. July 23, 2006.

11 Steele, Shelby. Interview. 'White Guilt' and the End of the Civil Rights Era.npr.com, March 5, 2006.

12 Mosteller, R.P. "The Duke Lacrosse Case, Innocence, and False Identifications. A Fundamental Failure to "Do Justice." Fordham Law Review. 76 (3): 1337-1412, 2007.

13 Garcia, Sandra. Jussie Smollett Charges Were Dropped Because Conviction Was Uncertain, Prosecutor Says. NY Times, March 30, 2019.

14 Riley, Jason. Hate Crime Hoaxes are More Common than You Think. Wall Street Journal, June 26, 2019.

15 Jussie Smollett: Timeline of the actor's alleged attack and arrest. BBC.com. February 12. 2020.

16 Al Sharpton demands answers in nascar noose probe.... Or Else!!! TMZ.com, June 23, 2020.

17 Triplett, Mike. Saints' Drew Brees draws backlash for 'disrespecting the flag' comment. ESPN.com, June 3, 2020.

18 Goldenberg, Susan. US election 2008: 'I want to cut his nuts out' - Jackson gaffe turns focus on Obama's move to the right. The Guardian, July 10, 2008.

19 Linderman, Juliet. Ben Carlson falls from grace in the city that once claimed him. Baltimore Sun, August 20, 2018.

20 Religion and Living Arrangements Around the World. Pew Research Center, December 12, 2019.

21 America's Families and Living Arrangements: 2020. US Census, retrieved February 8, 2021.

22 Children in single-parent families by race in the United States. Kidscount, retrieved February 2, 2021.

23 Sowell, Thomas. Discrimination and Disparities. Basic Books, 2019.

24 Number of people shot to death by the police in the United States from 2017 to 2020, by race. Statista, January 5, 2020.

25 Tibbitts, Lisa. The risk of being killed by a police officer is lower than you probably imagine. StarTribune, June 13, 2017

26 Walsh, Matt. WALSH: I Looked Up Every Case of An Unarmed Black Man Shot By Cops In 2019. Here's the Truth The Left Is Hiding. Dailywire, July 24, 2020.

27 2018 Law Enforcement Officers Feloniously Killed 2009-2018. Ucr.fbi.gov, retrieved February 5, 2021.

28 Officer Down Memorial Page. Odmp.org, retrieved February 5, 2021.

29 Known offender crosstabs. Ojjdp.gov, retrieved, January 25, 2021.

30 FBI:UCR 2017, 2018 arrests by race & ethnicity, retrieved February 28, 2021

31 Kass James. Obama shouldn't embrace race-rousing Sharpton. Chicago Tribune, April 16, 2014.

32 McDonald, Heather. Obama's Ferguson Sellout. The Washington Free Beacon July 11, 2016.

33 New Poll: Obama Poisoned Race Relations In America. Investors.com, November 4, 2014.

34 Number of people shot to death by the police in the United States from 2017 to 2020, by race. Statista, January 5, 2020.

35 Gonzalez, Mike. For Five Months, BLM Protesters Trashed America's Cities. Heritage.org, November 6, 2020.

36 Roos, Meghan. BLM Leader: We'll 'Burn' the System Down If U.S. Won't Give Us What We Want. Newsweek, June 25, 2020.

37 Cox, Chelsea. Fact check: Quotes from Democratic leaders about riots, unrest taken out of context. USA Today, January 15, 2021.

38 Mayor says task force will shape her $100M promise made during Seattle's Black Lives Matter protests — UPDATE. Capitol Hill Blog, September 28, 2020.

39 Taylor, Keeanga-Yamahtta. A Black Lives Matter Founder on Building Modern Movements. The New Yorker, January 18, 2021.

40 Ludwig, Hayden. ActBlue: The Left's Favorite "Dark Money" Machine. Capital Research, June 16, 2020.

41 Doran, Michael F. "Negro Slaves of the Five Civilized Tribes." Annals of the Association of American Geographers, vol. 68, no. 3, pp. 335–350, 1978.

42 Gates, Henry Louis. "How Many Slaves Landed in the U.S.?" Pbs.org, retrieved November 16, 2016.

43 McHugo, A Concise History of Sunnis & Shi'is. Saqi Books, 2018.

[44] Bufkin, Ellie. Biden faces backlash over vow to prioritize minority-owned businesses. KATV.com, January 12, 2021.

[45] Hightower, Kamaria. Equitable Communities Initiative Task Force Launches to Guide Historic $100 Million Investment in BIPOC Communities. Seattle.gov, October 14, 2020.

[46] Stanley, Thomas, Danko William. The Millionaire Next Door: The Surprising Secrets of America's Wealthy. Taylor Trade Publishing, 2010.

[47] Jacobs, Peter. Harvard is Being accused of treating Asians the Same Way it Treated Jews. Business Insider, December 4, 2014.

[48] Charlesworth, Tessa, Banaji, Mahzarin. Research: How Americans' Biases Are Changing (or Not) Over Time. Harvard Business Review, August 14, 2019.

[49] Flores, Andrew, Brown N.T. Taylor, Herman, Jody. Race and Ethnicity of Adults Who Identify as Transgender in the United States. UCLA School of Law, The Williams Institute, October 2016.

[50] Jackson, Mary. Washington state erases parents from the equation. World, November 13, 2020.

[51] Thomas, Jake. Delaying Puberty with the Help of the State. The Atlantic, October 22, 2014.

[52] Oregon. Parents' Rights in Education, retrieved February 9, 2021.

[53] Basic Rights Oregon. Oregon Health Plan Coverage for Gender Dysphoria. Basicrights.org, retrieved February 9, 2021.

[54] Smith, Steve. Gender Reassignment Surgery Is Now Available to Oregon Minors Without Parental Consent. Medical Daily, July 13, 2015.

[55] A new push to ban medical treatments for transgender children. The Economist, February 1, 2020.

[56] Chalk, Casey. Virginia Plans for All Public Schools to Allow Boys in Girls Bathrooms and Sleepovers. The Federalist, January 14, 2021.

[57] Schwartz, Yardena. Things are only getting worse. French Jews are Leaving Their Country. National Geographic, November 20, 2019.

[58] A Survey About Attitudes Towards Jews in America. Anti-Defamation League, 2016.

[59] Eagles. NBC Sports, July 7, 2020.

[60] Cohen, Seth. Nick Cannon's YouTube Show Causes Waves. Forbes, July 13, 2020.

[61] Reich, Aaron. Ilhan Omar voted 2019's anti-Semite of the year, Jerusalem Post, January 7, 2020.

[62] Connolly, Griffin. Rep. Rashida Tlaib defends Holocaust, Israel comments against critics. Rollcall, May 13, 2019.

[63] Mill, John Stuart, 1806-1873. The Subjection of Women. London: Longmans, Green, Reader, and Dyer, 1878.

[64] Radbil Sam. Tolerance in America: The Most Racist Cities in The United States. Rentable.co, April 25, 2016.

[65] Starbucks Showed This Short Film to Its Employees To Teach Them About Racial Bias. Now This, June 8, 2018.

[66] Kaufman, Scott Barry. Unraveling the Mindset of Victimhood. Scientific American, June 29, 2020.

[67] Jacobs, Emily. Jamaal Bowman calls capitalism 'slavery,' says Dems should follow 'Squad,' not Obama. NY Post, December 22, 2020.

[68] Hamren, Kelly. Social Justice, Critical Race Theory, Marxism, and Biblical Ethics. Christianity Today, July 3, 2020.

[69] Walton, S. Why the critical race theory concept of 'White supremacy' should not be dismissed by neo-Marxists: Lessons from contemporary Black radicalism. Power and Education, 12(1), 78–94, 2020.

[70] Subotnik, Daniel. "What's Wrong with Critical Race Theory: Reopening the Case for Middle Class Values," Cornell Journal of Law and Public Policy: Vol. 7: Iss. 3, Article 1, 1998.

[71] Curry, Tommy. Critical Race Theory. Encyclopedia Britannica, retrieved December 29, 2020.

[72] Pluckrose, Helen, Lindsay, James. Cynical Theories. Cynical Theories: How Activist Scholarship Made Everything about Race, Gender, and Identity—and Why This Harms Everybody. Pitchstone Publishing, August 25, 2020.

[73] Publications as predictors of racial and ethnic differences in NIH research awards. PLOS One, retrieved January 19, 2021.

[74] McWhorter, John. Losing the Race: Self-Sabotage in Black America. Harper Perennial, 2001.

[75] Cokley, Kevin. What Do We Know about the Motivation of African American Students? Challenging the "Anti-Intellectual" Myth. Harvard Educational Review 73. 524-558, 2003.

[76] Cokely, Kevin. The Myth of Black Anti-Intellectualism: A True Psychology of African American Students (Practical and Applied Psychology). Praeger, 2014.

[77] Gregory, Sophfronia Scott. The Hidden Hurdle. Talented black students find that one of the most insidious obstacles to achievement comes from a surprising source: their own peers. Time, March 16, 1992.

[78] Fryer, Roland, Smith, David-Austen. The Economics of Acting White. National Bureau of Economic Research, August 2003.

[79] Fryer, Roland, Smith, David-Austen. "Acting White" or Just Acting Rationally? Kellogg Insight, June 7, 2007.

[80] MacArdle, Mairead. African American History Museum Publishes Graphic Linking 'Rational Linear Thinking,' 'Nuclear Family' to White Culture. National Review, July 15, 2020.

[81] Kendi, Ibram X. How to be an Anti-Racist. One World, 2019.

[82] Critical Race Theory.Cyber.harvard.edu, retrieved December 29, 2020.

[83] Glazer, Nathan. Affirmative Discrimination. Harvard University Press, 1987.

[84] Pluckrose, Helen, Lindsay, James. Cynical Theories. Cynical Theories: How Activist Scholarship Made Everything about Race, Gender, and Identity—and Why This Harms Everybody, Pitchstone Publishing. August 25, 2020.

[85] Bell, Derrick. And We Are Not Saved: the elusive quest for racial justice. Perseus Books, 2008.

[86] Ross, S. Chapter 14: Critical Race Theory, Educational Equity, and Democracy in the US. Counterpoints, *355*, 209-225, 2010.

[87] Steinweis, Alan, E. Rachlin, Robert, D. Law in Nazi Germany: The Ideology, Opportunism, and the Perversion of Justice. Berghahn Books, 2013.

[88] Mahajan, N., Martinez, M., Gutierrez, N. L., Diesendruck, G., Banaji, M., & Santos, L. R. Retraction of Mahajan, Martinez, Gutierrez, Diesendruck, Banaji, & Santos (2011). Journal of Personality and Social Psychology, 106, 182, 2014.

[89] Barlett, Tom. Can We Really Measure Implicit Bias? Maybe Not. The Chronicle of Higher Education, January 5, 2017.

[90] Quattlebaum, Megan. Let's get real: Behavioral Realism, Implicit Bias, and the Reasonable Police Officer. Stanford Journal of Civil Rights and Civil Liberties, February 8, 2018.

[91] Ingle, Sarah. Kang Proposes Behavioral Realist Revision of Affirmative Action. University of Virginia Law, October 24, 2005.

[92] McDonald, Heather. Are We All Unconscious Racists? City-Journal, Autumn, 2017.

[93] White, Christopher. PBS attorney resigns after saying Trump voters' children should face 're-education camps.' ABC.WCTI12. January 14, 2021.

[94] Kendi, Ibram X. Pass an anti-Racist Constitutional Amendment. Politico, retrieved January 15, 2021.

[95] Sullivan, Andrew. A Glimpse at the Intersectional Left's Political Endgame. New York Magazine, November 15. 2019.

[96] Sanneh, Kelefa. The Fight to Redefine Racism. New York Magazine, August 12, 2019.

[97] Does legislation prohibit discrimination at work based on race/ethnicity? World Policy Center, 2020.

[98] Steele, Shelby. Interview. 'White Guilt' and the End of the Civil Rights Era. Npr.com, March 5, 2006.

[99] Hughes, Coleman. Sermon for Whites to Wash Away "Original Sin" Is Misguided Gospel of Anti-Racism. NY Post, December 1, 2020.

[100] Heller J. Rumors and Realities: Making Sense of HIV/AIDS Conspiracy Narratives and Contemporary Legends. American journal of public health, 105(1), e43–e50, 2015.

[101] Fruen, Lauren. Nation of Islam leader Louis Farrakhan calls the vaccine 'toxic waste' that will cause harm - as mistrust grows among black Americans with fewer than 25% saying they will get the shot. Daily Mail, December 15, 2020.

[102] Selmi, Michael L., The Evolution of Employment Discrimination Law: Changed Doctrine for Changed Social Conditions. GWU Law School Public Law Research Paper No. 2014-8, GWU Legal Studies Research Paper No. 2014-8, 2014.

[103] What Are the Top 10 Reasons People Get Fired? Spiggle law, retrieved January 4, 2021.

[104] Sowell, Thomas. Discrimination and Disparities. Basic Books, 2019.

[105] Labor Force Statistics from the Current Population Survey. Bureau of Labor Statistics, retrieved December 27, 2020.

[106] Indicator 27: Educational Attainment. National Center for Educational Statistics, retrieved January 4, 2021.

[107] Dropout rates. National Center for Education Statistics, 2018.

[108] Poll finds at least half of Black Americans say they have experienced racial discrimination in their jobs and from the police. Harvard School of Public Health. October 24, 2017.

[109] Tomaskovic-Devey D. When Discrimination Goes to Court. Contexts;17(3):56-58, 2018

[110] Bertrand, Marianne, Mullainathan, Sendhil. Are Emily and Greg More Employable than Lakisha and Jamal? American Economic Review, 991-1013, September 4, 2004.

[111] BETA Report: Unconscious Bias in Recruitment. Video. Australia National Government, July 11, 2017.

[112] Axt, J. R., Ebersole, C. E., & Nosek, B. A. An unintentional, robust, and replicable pro-Black bias in social judgment. Social Cognition, 2016.

[113] Moss P, Tilly C. Stories Employers Tell: Race, Skill and Hiring in America. New York: Russell Sage Foundation, 2001.

[114] Turczynski, Bart. Resume Bias: Gender, Names, Ethnicity [2020 Study]. Zety.com, October 13, 2020.

[115] Critical Race Theory: On the New Ideology of Race. Manhattan Institute, December 16, 2020.

[116] Monllos, Kristina. Inside agencies, men and women still struggle with the fallout of #MeToo. Digiday, January 2, 2020.

[117] Employment and Discrimination: Exploring the Climate of Workplace Discrimination from 1997 to 2018. Paychex, August 1, 2019.

[118] Stobierski, Tim. Average Salary by Education Level: The Value of a College Degree. Northeastern University, June 2, 2020.

[119] Tate, Emily. Graduation Rates and Race. Inside Higher Ed, April 26, 2017.

[120] Women and Minorities in the Science and Engineering Workforce. NSF.gov, retrieved October 12, 2020.

[121] Bowles, Hannah Riley. Three things you should know about pay discrimination. Harvard Kennedy School, January 30, 2020.

[122] Blake, John. How an internet mob falsely painted a Chipotle employee as racist. CNN.com, May 27, 2019.

[123] Siapera, Eugenia. Organised and Ambient Digital Racism: Multidirectional Flows in the Irish Digital Sphere. Open Library of Humanities, February 2019.

[124] Keith C. Burris: Primed for outrage. Pittsburgh Gazette, January 29, 2019.

[125] Race & Justice News: One Third of Black Men Have Convictions. The Sentencing Project, October 10, 2017.

[126] Paulhus, D., Duncan, J.H., & Yik, M. (2002). Patterns of shyness in East-Asian and European-heritage students. Journal of Research in Personality, 36, 442-462.

[127] Sturm, S. Second Generation Employment Discrimination: A Structural Approach. Columbia Law Review, 101(3), 458-568, 2001.

[128] Powell, John, A. University of Arkansas Clinton School of Public Service & Center on Community Philanthropy, 2013.

[129] Powell, G. N., & Butterfield, D. A. The "Good Manager": Did Androgyny Fare Better in the 1980s? Group & Organization Studies, 14(2), 216–233, 1989.

[130] Horowitz, Juliana, Brown, Anna, Cox, Kiana. The role of race and ethnicity in American's personal lives. Pew Social Trends, April 9, 2019.

[131] McKenna, Barbara. The color of Black: Professor explores racial identity in college students. Stanford Graduate School of Education, retrieved July 14, 2020.

[132] Baldwin, J.A. African self-consciousness and the mental health of African-Americans. Journal of BlackStudies,15,177-19, 1984

[133] Parham, T. A., Cycles of Psychological Nigrescence. The Counseling Psychologist, 17(2), 187–226, 1989.

[134] Steele, Shelby. A Dream Deferred: the second betrayal of black freedom in America. Harper Collins, 2009.

[135] Sellers, R. M., & Shelton, J. N. The role of racial identity in perceived racial discrimination. Journal of Personality and Social Psychology, 84(5), 1079–1092, 2003.

[136] Michael T. Schmitt & Nyla R. Branscombe. The Meaning and Consequences of Perceived Discrimination in Disadvantaged and Privileged Social Groups, European Review of Social Psychology, 12:1, 167-199, 2002.

[137] Greenwald, A. G., & Pettigrew, T. F. With malice toward none and charity for some: Ingroup favoritism enables discrimination. American Psychologist, 69(7), 669–684, 2014.

[138] A Conversation with Clarence Thomas. Library of Congress, April 13, 2018.

[139] Taylor, Jim. Perception is not Reality. Psychology Today, August 5, 2019.

[140] Hamel, Liz, Lopez, Lunna, Manana, Cailey, Artiga, Samantha, Brodie, Mollyann. KFF/The Undefeated Survey on Race and Health. Kff.org, October 13, 2020.

[141] Chamorro-Pemuzic, Tomas. Science explains why unconscious bias training won't reduce workplace racism. Here's what will. Fast Company, June 12, 2020.

[142] McDonald, Heather. The False 'Science' of Implicit Bias. Wall Street Journal, October 9, 2017.

[143] Washington, Jesse. Black American overwhelming say unconscious bias is a major barrier in their lives. The undefeated.com, October 16, 2020.

[144] Schwartz, Joel. Roots of unconscious prejudice affect 90 to 95 percent of people, psychologists demonstrate at press conference. University of Washington News, September 29, 1998.

[145] Johnson, Theodore, R. Black-on Black Racism: The Hazards of Implicit bias. The Atlantic, December 26, 2014.

[146] Handelsman, Jo, Sakraney, Natasha. Implicit Bias. Obamawhitehouse.archives.gov, 2015.

[147] Blanton, H., & Jaccard, J. Unconscious racism: A concept in pursuit of a measure. Annual Review of Sociology, 34, 277–297, 2008.

[148] Hutson, Matthew, Implicit Biases Toward Race and Sexuality Have Decreased. Scientific American, April 1, 2019

[149] Blanton, H., & Jaccard, J. Unconscious racism: A concept in pursuit of a measure. Annual Review of Sociology, 34, 277–297, 2008.

[150] Hutson, Matthew, Implicit Biases Toward Race and Sexuality Have Decreased. Scientific American, April 1, 2019

[151] Coutts, Alexander. Racial bias around the world. osf.io, June 24, 2020.

[152] Seidman, Gwendolyn. Why do we like people who are similar to us? Psychology Today, December 18, 2018.

[153] Barlett, Tom. Can We Really Measure Implicit Bias? Maybe Not. The Chronicle of Higher Education, January 5, 2017.

[154] Mason, Betsy. Curbing implicit bias: what works and what doesn't. Knowable Magazine, June 4, 2020.

[155] Banaji, M. R., & Greenwald, A.G. Blindspot: Hidden biases of good people. New York, NY: Random House, 2013.

[156] Mitchell, G., & Tetlock, P. E. Popularity as a poor proxy for utility: The case of implicit prejudice. In S. O. Lilienfeld & I. D. Waldman (Eds.), Psychological science under scrutiny: Recent challenges and proposed solutions (p. 164–195). Wiley Blackwell, 2017.

[157] McDonald, Heather. Are We All Unconscious Racists? City-Journal, Autumn, 2017.

[158] California Legislature Confronts Racial Discrimination in New Criminal Justice Reform Package. American Bar Association, October 28, 2020.

[159] Dobbin, Frank, Kalev, Alexandra. Why Corporate Diversity Initiatives Fail? Harvard Business Review, July-August 2016.

[160] Bezrukova, K., Spell, C. S., Perry, J. L., & Jehn, K. A. A meta-analytical integration of over 40 years of research on diversity training evaluation. Psychological Bulletin, 11, 1227-1274, 2016.

[161] Gonzalez, Mike. For Five Months, BLM Protesters Trashed America's Cities. Heritage.org, November 6, 2020.

[162] Paluck, E.L., Green, D.P Prejudice Reduction: What Works" A Review and Assessment of Research and Practice. Annual Review of Psychology. Vol 60:339-367, January 10, 2009.

[163] Stillman, J., Why Your Gender Equality Training Won't Work (and What You Should Do Instead). Inc.com, October 23, 2018.

[164] University of Arkansas. Research examines link between unconscious bias and its effect on behavior. University of Arkansas News, July 2019.

[165] Rhodes, D.L. Gender stereotypes and unconscious bias. Handbook of Research on Gender and Leadership (pp. 287-302.). In S.R. Madsen (Ed). Cheltenham, England: Edward Elgar Publishing, 2017.

[166] Clark, P. The big problem with unconscious bias training. Financial Times, October 21, 2018.

[167] Lipman, How Diversity Training fails Women and Infuriates Men. Time.com, January 25, 2018.

[168] MacArdle, Mairead. African American History Museum Publishes Graphic Linking 'Rational Linear Thinking,' 'Nuclear Family' to White Culture. National Review, July 15, 2020.

[169] Markovich, Matt. Segregated diversity training session at Seattle City Hall stirs controversy. KOMOnews, July 9, 2020.

[170] Clarence Page: Let's not make race and culture too hot for our teachers to handle. The Philadelphia Tribune, February 14, 2021.

[171] Moya, M., Glick, P., Expósito, F., de Lemus, S., & Hart, J. It's for Your Own Good: Benevolent Sexism and Women's Reactions to Protectively Justified Restrictions. Personality and Social Psychology Bulletin, 33(10), 1421–1434, 2007.

[172] Becker, J., & Wright, S. Yet another dark side of chivalry: Benevolent sexism undermines and hostile sexism motivates collective action for social change. Journal of Personality and Social Psychology, *101* (1), 62-77, 2011.

[173] Esposito, Luigi; Romano, Victor Benevolent Racism: Upholding Racial Inequality in the Name of Black Empowerment. *The* Western Journal of Black Studies, Summer 2014.

[174] Elder, Larry. The secret story of blacks' success. Baltimore Sun, September 8, 2004.

[175] 21.3 % of U.S. Population Participates in Government Assistance Programs Each Month. US Census, May 28, 2015.

[176] Tanner, Michael, Hughes, Charles. The Work vs. Welfare Tradeoff: 2013. Cato, 2013.

[177] Irving, Shelley. How Long Do People Receive Assistance? US Census, May 28, 2014.

[178] Indicators of Welfare Dependence. Fourteenth Report to Congress. US Dept. of Health and Human Services, 2015.

[179] Walter Williams: Suffer No Fools. Video. Free to Choose Network, December 29, 2015.

[180] James, Kay. Why we must be bold on welfare reform. Heritage.org, May 12, 2018.

[181] Cashin, Sheryll. The Failures of Integration: How Race and Class are Undermining the American Dream. New York: Public Affairs, 2004.

[182] Heilman, M. E., Block, C. J., & Stathatos, P. The affirmative action stigma of incompetence: Effects of performance information ambiguity. Academy of Management Journal, 40(3), 603-625, 1997.

[183] Heilman, Madeline, Simon, Michael, C., Repper, David P. Intentionally Favored, Unintentionally Harmed? Impact of Sex-Based Preferential Selection on Self-Perceptions and Self-Evaluations. Journal of Applied Psychology, February 1987.

[184] Sacks, David, Thiel, Peter. The Case Against Affirmative Action. Stanford Magazine, September/October 1996.

[185] McDonald, Heather. The Diversity Delusion. St. Martin's Press, 2018.

[186] Fone, Zachary, Sabia, Joseph, Cesure, Sabia. Do Minimum Wage Increases Reduce Crime? National Bureau of Economic Research, October 2020.

[187] Estimated number of arrests by offense and race, 2019: all ages. Office of Justice and Juvenile Delinquency Prevention, retrieved December 30, 2020.

[188] William, Walter, E. The Effects of Minimum Wage. Libertypen, You Tube, January 18, 2015.

[189] Nordin, M., Almén, D. Long-term unemployment and violent crime. Empirical Economics 52, 1–29, 2017.

[190] Horowitz, Juliana. Most Americans say the legacy of slavery still affects black people in the U.S. today. Pew Research, June 17, 2019.

[191] Desmond-Harris, Jenee. Here's where "white" Americans have the highest percentage of African ancestry. Vox, February 20, 2015.

[192] Gal, Shayanna, Kiersz, Andy, Mark, Michelle, Su, Ruobing, Ward, Maguerite. 26 simple charts to show friends and family who aren't convinced racism is still a problem in America. Business Insider, July 8, 2020.

[193] Hamel, Liz, Lopez, Lunna, Manana, Cailey, Artiga, Samantha, Brodie, Mollyann. KFF/The Undefeated Survey on Race and Health. Kff.org, October 13, 2020.

[194] Loury, Glenn. One by One from the Inside Out: Essays and Reviews on Race and Responsibility in America. Free Press, 1995.

[195] Douglass, Frederick, What the Black Man Wants. Utc.iath.virginai.edu, retrieved January 7, 2021.

[196] Williams, Walter. Ammunition for Poverty Pimps. Walterewilliams.com, retrieved January 13, 2021.

[197] Sowell, Thomas. Poverty pimp's poem. Tulsaworld, November 4, 1998.

[198] Noted Black Conservative Warren, Steve. Economist, Opponent of 'the Welfare State', Prof. Walter E. Williams Dead at 84. CBNews, December 12, 2020.

[199] Academic Achievement in the District of Columbia Public and Public Charter Schools. DCPCSB.org, November 22, 2019.

[200] Cherry, Robert. What would Biden do when it comes to charter schools? Thehill.com, September 9, 2020.

[201] State of the Union Response: Charter Schools Key to Addressing Income Inequality. National Alliance for Public Charter Schools, January 29, 2014.

[202] Biddle, Rishawn. When Black Kids Don't Matter. California Policy Center, August 15, 2016.

[203] Making Black Lives Matter at School. Socialistworker.org, February 1, 2018.

[204] Antonucci, Mike, Analysis: Tracking the NEA's and AFT's $43 Million in Donations to PACs, Advocacy Organizations, Nonprofits — and the State Engagement Fund? 74million.org, retrieved January 26, 2021.

[205] Hawkins, Vesia. Do you hear what I hear. Volume & Light, 2017.

[206] Biddle, Rishawn. When Black Kids Don't Matter. California Policy Center, August 15, 2016.

[207] Ryan, Julia. American Schools vs. the World: Expensive, Unequal, Bad at Math. The Atlantic, December 3, 2013.

[208] Ikhlas, Saleem. Everything You Need to Know About the NAACP's Stance on Charter Schools. Education Post, July 31, 2017.

[209] Charles, Brian, J. How Charter Schools Lost Democrats' Support. Governing.com, April 2019.

[210] The Project 1619 Resource Page. NEA EdJustice, retrieved January 17, 2021.

[211] Webinar: The 1619 Project and Activities for Student Engagement. The Pulitzer Center, March 24, 2020.

[212] Williams, Walter. Opinion: The true plight of blacks in America. The Item, June 10, 2020.

[213] Truong, Debbie. D.C. Schools Show Improvement — But Also Persistent Challenges, Report Says. NPR, January 16, 2020.

[214] Black Lives Matter 13 Guiding Principles. DC Area Educators for Social Justice, February 2020.

[215] Charles, Brian. How Charter Schools Lost Democrats' Support. Governing, April 2019.

[216] Cherry, Robert. What would Biden do when it comes to charter schools? Thehill.com, September 9, 2020

[217] Talking with Glenn Loury about "Woke" Culture and Racism Today. Video. Ayn Rand Institute, January 20, 2021.

[218] Ho, Sally. AP: Billionaires fuel US charter school movement. Detroit News, July 16, 2018.

[219] Rev. Sharpton: Education problems are a 'five-alarm' fire. Citizen Stewart, October 26, 2020.

[220] Ujifusa, Andrew. Untangling the Role of Trump, Unions, and Politics in School Reopening Decisions. Education Week, October 13, 2020.

[221] Green, Erica. Surge of student suicides pushes Las Vegas Schools to reopen. NY Times, January 24, 2021.

[222] McDonald, Kerry. Youth Depression, Suicide Increasing During Pandemic Response. Foundation for Economic Education, January 27, 2021.

[223] Kogan, Vladimir, Prasad, Vinay. Op-Ed: Public Schools Should (Almost Always) Stay Open. MedPage Today, Jan. 12, 2021.

[224] Wigfall, Catrin. Joe Biden and teachers' union share same feelings on charter schools. Center of the American Experiment, September 21, 2020.

[225] Sweet, Lynn, Issa, Nader, Speilman, Fran. Biden signals support for CTU's COVID-19 safety concerns as top union chief briefs White House. Chicago Sun Times, January 25, 2021.

[226] Teachers Union. OpenSecrets.org, retrieved February 4, 2021.

[227] Analysis: How 18 Top Charter School Networks Are Adapting to Online Education, and What Other Schools Can Learn From Them. The74million.org.

[228] Rebarber, Ted; Zgainer, Alison Consoletti. Annual Survey of America's Charter Schools 2014. Center for Education Reform, February 2014.

[229] Gregory, Sophfronia Scott. The Hidden Hurdle. Talented black students find that one of the most insidious obstacles to achievement comes from a surprising source: their own peers. Time, March 16, 1992.

[230] Fryer, Roland, Smith, David-Austen. The Economics of Acting White. National Bureau of Economic Research, August 2003.

[231] Riley, Jason. Please Stop Helping Us. Encounter Books, 2016.

[232] Zahneis, Meghan. Why Has Black-Student Enrollment Fallen? Chronicle.com, August 18, 2019.

[233] College Enrollment & Student Demographic Statistics. Educationdata.org, retrieved January 4, 2020.

[234] Casteel, Clifton. Teacher Student Interactions and Race in Integrated School Environments. Journal of Educational Research 92, 115-120, 1998.

[235] Auxier, Brooke, Anderson, Monica, Perrin, Andrew, Turner, Erica. Parenting Children in the Age of Screens. Pew Research Center, July 28, 2020.

[236] Alice Park. The Tiger Mom Effect Is Real, Says Large Study. Time, May 5, 2104.

[237] "Why Family Income Differences Don't Explain the Racial Gap in SAT scores. Journal of Blacks in Higher Education, no 20, Summer 1998.

[238] Ramey, Valerie. Is there a "Tiger Mother" Effect? Time Use Across Ethnic Groups. UC San Diego Economics in Action, March 2011.

[239] Stobierski, Tim. Average Salary by Education Level: The Value of a College Degree. Northeastern University, June 2, 2020.

[240] Tate, Emily. Graduation Rates and Race. Inside Higher Ed, April 26, 2017.

[241] Wodtke G. T. The Impact of Education on Inter-Group Attitudes: A Multiracial Analysis. Social psychology quarterly, 75(1), 2012.

[242] McHugo, John. A Concise History of Sunnis & Shia'is. Saqi Books, 2018.

[243] Germany is popular in Israel, study says. DW.com, 2014.

[244] Brown, Sarah Drake, Patrick, John. History Education in the United States: A Survey of Teacher Certification and State-Based Standards and Assessments for Teachers and Students. Organizations of American Historians, April 18, 2013.

[245] Mackaman, Tom. An interview with historian James McPherson on the New York Times' 1619 Project. WSWS.org, November 2019.

[246] Wood, Peter. 1620: A Critical Response to the 1619 Project. Encounter Books, 2020.

[247] Twelve Scholars Critique the 1619 Project and the New York Times Magazine Editor Responds. History News Network, January 6, 2020.

[248] The Fatal Flaw of the 1619 Project Curriculum. The American Revolution Institute, August 14, 2020.

[249] Interview with Peter Wood. Ward Scott Files, November 25, 2020.

[250] Kurtz. Stanley. A Book for Our *Times*: Peter Wood's 1620 Skewers 1619 Project. National Review, November 16, 2020.

[251] Adam Silverstein (Ed). Project 1619. NY Times Magazine, August 18, 2019.

[252] Gates, Henry Louis. 100 Amazing Facts About the Negro. Pantheon, 2017.

[253] Schweninger, L. (1990). Prosperous Blacks in the South, 1790-1880. The American Historical Review, *95*(1), 31-56.

[254] Statistics on Slavery. Faculty.weber.edu, retrieved February 1, 2021.

[255] Gates, Henry Lewis. "Did Black People Own Slaves." The Root, 2013.

[256] Milikh, Arthur. 1776, not 1619. City-Journal, October 29, 2019.

[257] Jones, Tom. A deeper look into the controversy of The New York Times' '1619 Project.' Poynter, October 14, 2020.

[258] 1619 Project Resources. Pulitzer Center, retrieved December 27, 2020.

[259] Pavlu, George. Recalling Africa's harrowing tale of its first slavers – The Arabs – as UK Slave Trade Abolition is commemorated. New Africa, March 27, 2018.

[260] Wilenz, Sean A Matter of Facts. The Atlantic, January 22, 2020.

[261] Guelzo, Allen. The 1619 Projects Outrageous, Lying Slander of Abraham Lincoln. Heritage.org, May 5, 2020.

[262] Mackaman, Tom. The 1619 Chronicles. NY Times, November 14, 2019.

[263] Jones, Tom. A deeper look into the controversy of The New York Times' '1619 Project.' Poynter, October 14, 2020.

[264] Constantin A. Human Subject Research: International and Regional Human Rights Standards. Health and human rights, 20(2), 137–148, 2018.

[265] Kaufman, Scott Barry. Unraveling the Mindset of Victimhood. Scientific American. June 29, 2020.

[266] Harmata, Claudia. Martellus Bennett Says 'the NFL Is Racist': League 'Was Built on the Backs of Black Athletes.' People, June 4, 2020.

[267] Lauterback, David. Michael Bennett thinks the NCAA is slavery. The Comeback, October 11, 2016.

[268] Starr, Jemaine Terrell. Jamaal Bowman Wants to Reimagine the Democratic Party. The Root, December 21, 2021.

[269] Cwik, Chris. Rutgers senior Geo Baker rips NCAA over athlete rights: 'Modern day slavery.' Yahoo News, January 30, 2021.

[270] Interview with White House Correspondent Yamichi Alcindor. MSNBC, February 7, 2021.

[271] Frequently Asked Questions Regarding Unaccompanied Children. Department of Health and Human Services, Feb. 8, 2021.

[272] Malone, Justin. Uncle Tom. Movie, 2020.

[273] Robinson, Frederick D. The rhetoric of victimization that is paralyzing black America. Chicago Tribune, Jan. 14, 1991.

[274] 1776unites.com

[275] Malone, Justin. Uncle Tom. Movie, 2020.

[276] The Universal Declaration of Human Rights, 1948.

[277] Twelve Scholars Critique the 1619 Project and the New York Times Magazine Editor Responds. History News Network, January 6, 2020.

[278] The warm cloak of victimhood | Glenn Loury & John McWhorter [The Glenn Show]. Bloggingheads.tv, Dec. 11, 2020.

[279] Robinson, Frederick D. The rhetoric of victimization that is paralyzing black America. Chicago Tribune, Jan. 14, 1991.

[280] Naseem, Saba. How Much U.S. History Do Americans Actually Know? Less Than You Think. Smithsonian Magazine, May 28,2015.

[281] American lack of foreign knowledge 'dangerous.' Times of Higher Education, December 2, 2005.

[282] Kendi, Ibram X. How to be an Anti-Racist. One World, 2019.

[283] Asante, M. The Afrocentric Idea in Education. The Journal of Negro Education 60 (2), 170-180, 1991.

[284] East Africa's forgotten slave trade. DW.com, retrieved January 5, 2021.

[285] Madany, Bassam, Michael. The Veiled Genocide" A Forgotten Historic Tragedy, May 22, 2018.

[286] Ibid.

[287] Hair, P. The Enslavement of Koelle's Informants. The Journal of African History, 6(2), 193-203, 1965.

[288] Slavery among the Igbo. American Historical Society, historians.org. retrieved July 23, 2020.

[289] 'My Nigerian great-grandfather sold slaves.' BBC.com, July 16, 2020.

[290] Historical Survey – Slave Owning Societies. Encyclopedia Britannica, retrieved July 24, 2020.

[291] Nwaubani, A.T. The Descendants of Slaves in Nigeria Fight for Equality. New York Magazine, July 19, 2019.

[292] Renee C. Redman, The League of Nations and the Right to be Free from Enslavement: The First Human Right to Be Recognized as Customary International Law - Freedom: Beyond the United States, 70 Chi.-Kent L. Rev. 759, 1994.

[293] Sowell, Thomas. The Scapegoat for Strife in the Black Community. National Review, July 7, 2015.

[294] Crenshaw, Kimberle. "Demarginalizing the Intersection of Race and Sex: A Black Feminist Critique of Antidiscrimination Doctrine, Feminist Theory and Antiracist Politics," University of Chicago Legal Forum: Vol. 1989, Article 8, 1989.

[295] Carbado, Devon, Gulati, Mito. Acting White. Oxford University Press, 2015.

[296] Macrae, C. N., Bodenhausen, G. V., & Milne, A. B. The dissection of selection in person perception: Inhibitory processes in social stereotyping. Journal of Personality and Social Psychology, 69, 397-407, 1995.

[297] The Conversation (2016, February 4). Intersectionality: how gender interacts with other social identities to shape bias. Author.

[298] Krenshaw, Kimberle. 'Framing Affirmative Action", 105 Mich. L. Rev. First Impressions 123 (2006).

[299] Button, J., Bakker, R., & Rienzo, B. A. (2006). White women and affirmative action in employment in six southern cities. The Social Science Journal, 43(2), 297–302.

[300] Lublin, Gus. Admissions Officer: Here's What they Don't Tell You About Getting Into an Ivy League Business School. Business Insider, October 13, 2012.

[301] Kowarski, Ilana. How Gender Influences College Admissions. US News, November 2, 2018.

[302] White Privilege Checklist. Arizona State University, retrieved January 9, 2021

[303] Kendi, Ibram X. How to be an Anti-Racist. One World, 2019.

[304] Yang, Jiayun. China's plan to relax immigration rules spurs all sorts of hateful comments from nationalistic Chinese. Supchina.com, March 6, 2020.

[305] Benjamin, R. The Bizarre Classroom of Dr. Leonard Jeffries. The Journal of Blacks in Higher Education, (2), 91-96, 1993.

[306] O'Connell, Scott. Free speech on campus? It's 'complicated,' say college officials. Telegram.com, December 15, 2019.

[307] Stossel, John, McDonald, Heather. Campus Free Speech Crisis. City-Journal.org, April 30, 2018.

[308] Arria, Michael. Students at two universities just voted to divest from Israel. Mondoweiss, September 30, 2020.

[309] Bosco, David. Fire with Fire. The Harvard Crimson, November 9, 1994.

[310] A Survey About Attitudes Towards Jews in America. Anti-Defamation League, 2016.

[311] Sanneh, Kelefa. The Fight to Redefine Racism. New York Magazine, August 12, 2019.

[312] Grabmeier, Jeff. Research Reveals Massive Extent of Slavery Between Muslims, Christians For Three Centuries. OSU.edu, March 8, 2010.

[313] Madany, Bassam, Michael. The Veiled Genocide" A Forgotten Historic Tragedy, May 22, 2018.

[314] Kendi, Ibram X. How to be an Anti-Racist. One World, 2019.

[315] Sullivan, Andrew. A Glimpse at the Intersectional Left's Political Endgame. New York Magazine, November 15. 2019.

[316] Bacon, James. Kendi's Brand of "Anti-Racism" is Unconstitutional. Bacon's Rebellion, September 25, 2020.

[317] Hughes, Coleman. How to be an Anti-intellectual. City-Journal, October 27, 2019.

[318] Diangelo, Robin, White Fragility. Beacon Press, 2018.

[319] Banner, Stuart. How the Indians Lost their Land. Harvard University Press, 2007

[320] Brush, Kathleen. Racism and anti-Racism in the World: Before and after 1945. December 7, 2020.

[321] Hughes, Coleman. Sermon for Whites to Wash Away "Original Sin" Is Misguided Gospel of Anti-Racism. NY Post, December 1, 2020.

[322] McWhorter, John. The Dehumanizing Condescension of White Fragility. The Atlantic, July 15, 2020.

[323] Hughes, Coleman. Sermon for Whites to Wash Away "Original Sin" Is Misguided Gospel of Anti-Racism. NY Post, December 1, 2020.

[324] Harmata, Claudia. Martellus Bennett Says 'the NFL Is Racist': League 'Was Built on the Backs of Black Athletes.' People, June 4, 2020.

[325] Hamel, Liz, Lopez, Lunna, Manana, Cailey, Artiga, Samantha, Brodie, Mollyann. KFF/The Undefeated Survey on Race and Health. Kff.org, October 13, 2020.

[326] Papke, D. Heretics in the Temple: Americans Who Reject the Nation's Legal Faith. NYU Press, 1998.

[327] Balk, Gene. Poverty in Seattle, What the 2014 Community Survey tells us. University of Washington, October 29, 2015.

[328] Rantz. Jason. Rantz: City of Seattle hired a former pimp, but will fire up to 100 cops. Mynorthwest, September 24, 2020.

[329] Thrush, Glen. Revved Up. Politico. August 21, 2014.

[330] Markovich, Matt. Price tag for new city contract with Seattle 'street czar' draws scrutiny. Komonews, September 25, 2020.

[331] Chapman, Michael. Seattle Police Chief: There Are 'Rapes, Robberies' and 'We're Not Able to Get to' Them. CNSNews.com, June 12, 2020.

[332] Seattle, Wa Crime Analytics. Neighborhoodscout.com, retrieved January 28, 2021.

[333] Fone, Zachary, Sabia, Joseph, Cesure, Sabia. Do Minimum Wage Increases Reduce Crime? National Bureau of Economic Research, October 2020.

[334] Seattle/King County Point in time count of people experiencing homelessness. All Home, 2020.

[335] Rufo, Christopher. Crimes of Survival. City-Journal, January 2, 2019.

[336] Seattle, Wa Crime Analytics. Neighborhoodscout.com, retrieved January 28, 2021.

[337] Kroman, David. Misdemeanor arrests decline in Seattle as racial disparities remain, Crosscut, October 25, 2018.

[338] Sandberg, Erica. After Proposition 47: Crime and No Consequences in California. National Review, January 30, 2018.

[339] McQuillan, Lawrence. California Property Crime Surge Is Unintended Consequence of Proposition 47. Independent Institute. June 28, 2018.

[340] Rufo, Christopher. "Burn it Down" City-Journal, Autumn, 2020.

[341] Herzog, Katie. King County Among the Least Politically Tolerant Communities in the U.S. The Stranger, March 4, 2019.

[342] Bernstein, Maxine. 'What are we marching for?' Protesters and observers wonder alike in Portland. Oregon Live, January 24, 2021

[343] Gazaway, Wright. Portland Mayor Ted Wheeler responds to criticism of protests, police. KATU.com. October 14, 2020.

[344] Portland Police Shootings and Deaths in Custody: 1992-December 2020. Portlandcopwatch.com, retrieved Janaury 23, 2021.

[345] Drug War Statistics. Drugpolicy.org, retrieved February 5, 2021.

[346] Achen, Paris. Report: Disparity in drug convictions has declined. The Astorian, December 4, 2018.

[347] Oregon trends with U.S. in accelerated drug overdoses. Osteopathic physicians and surgeons, December 23, 2020.

[348] Trail Blazers. The Economist, February 13, 2021.

[349] Average drug seller doesn't make minimum wage, says anti-drug web site. CW39.com, December 14, 2014.

[350] Stossel, John. End the Drug War, Save Black America. Reason, March 17, 2011.

[351] Achen, Paris. Report: Disparity in drug convictions has declined. The Astorian, December 4, 2018.

[352] Known offender crosstabs. Ojjdp.gov, retrieved, January 28, 2021.

[353] Estimated number of arrests by offense and race, 2019: all ages. Office of Justice and Juvenile Delinquency Prevention, retrieved December 30, 2020.

[354] California Legislature Confronts Racial Discrimination in New Criminal Justice Reform Package. American Bar Association, October 28,2020.

[355] Racial Disparities in California Arrests, Public Policy Institute of California, retrieved February 6, 2021.

[356] McDonald, Heather. The Illegal Alien Crime Wave, City-Journal, Winter, 2004.

[357] Von Spakovsky, Hans. Crimes by Illegal Immigrants are Widespread Across US –Sanctuaries Shouldn't Shield Them, Heritage.org, September 3, 2019.

[358] Raphelson, Samantha, Hobson, Jeremy. California Sanctuary Law Divides State In Fierce Immigration Debate. Npr.org, October 17, 2018.

[359] White, Crisjen. Living in Fear: Understanding the Importance of Sanctuary Cities. Freedom and Citizenship, retrieved Janaury 30, 2021.

[360] Saccheti, Maria. Criminal immigrants reoffend at higher rates than ICE has suggested, Boston Globe, June 4, 2016.

[361] McDonald, Heather. The Illegal Alien Crime Wave. City-Journal, Winter, 2004.

[362] Haverluck, Michael. 80% of illegals released by sanctuary cities repeat crimes. Onenewsnow, October 26, 2019.

[363] False Claim: In 2018, 10,150 Americans were killed by illegal immigrants, while 194 Americans were killed in mass shootings. Reuters, February 27, 2020.

[364] Williams, Pete. Non-citizens account for 64% of federal arrests. NBC News, August 22, 2019.

[365] Bernstein, Leandra. Most fentanyl is now trafficked across US-Mexico border, not from China. ABC WJLA.com, July 16, 2019.

[366] Biers, David. 77% of Drug Traffickers Are U.S. Citizens, Not Illegal Immigrants. CATO, July 3, 2019.

[367] Overdose Death Rates. National Institute of Drug Abuse, retrieved February 6, 2021.

[368] Overdose Deaths Accelerating During COVID-19. CDC.gov, December 17, 2020.

[369] The Opioid Crisis and the Black/African American Population: An urgent Issue. SAMHSA.gov, retrieved. February 6, 2021.

370 Lopez, German. When a drug epidemic's victims are white. Vox, April 4, 2017.

371 Miroff, Nick, Sacchetti, Maria, New Biden rules for ICE point to fewer arrests and deportations, and a more restrained agency. Texas Tribune, February 7, 2021.

372 Alcindor Links 'White Supremacy' to Trump 'Torturing' Illegal Immigrants. MSNBC, February 7, 2021.

373 Hernandez, Tanya Kateri, Afrodescendants, Law, and Race in Latin America. Book Chapter, "Law and Race in Latin America," in Handbook of Law and Society in Latin America, eds. Tatiana Alfonso, Karina Ansolabehere, and Rachel Sieder. Fordham Law Legal Studies Research Paper No. 3589793, 2019.

374 Rahier, Jean Muteba. Blackness in the Andes: Ethnographic Vignettes of Cultural Politics in the Time of Multiculturalism. Palgrave Macmillan, 2014.

375 Rio violence: Police killings reach record high in 2019. BBC, Janaury 20, 2020.

376 Ilhan Omar. Twitter, March 12, 2020.

377 Fryer, Ronald G. An Empirical Analysis of Racial Differences in Police Use of Force. Harvard.edu, July 2017.

378 Johnson, David J. Tress, Burkel, Nicole, Carley Taylor, Carley, Cesario, Joseph. Officer characteristics and racial disparities in fatal officer-involved shootings. Proceedings of the National Academy of Sciences, 116 (32) 15877-15882, August 2019.

379 How Informed are Americans about Race and Policing? Skeptic Research Center. CUPES-007, February 20, 2021.

380 Bolhken, Donald. What do the statistics, not the stereotypes, about killings by the police tell us? Des Moines Register, June 29, 2020.

381 Stinson, Philip, Wentzlof, Chloe. On-Duty Shootings: Police Officers Charged with Murder or Manslaughter, 2005-2019. Bowling Green University, Police Integrity Research Group, 2019.

382 Mann, Brian, Baker, Elizabeth. Black Protest Leaders To White Allies: 'It's Our Turn To Lead Our Own Fight'. NPR, September 22, 2020.

383 Statistical Briefing Book. Estimated number of arrests by offense and race, 2019, retrieved February 11, 2021.

384 2018 Law Enforcement Officers Feloniously Killed 2009-2018. Ucr.fbi.gov, retrieved February 5, 2021.

385 Officer Down Memorial Page. Odmp.org, retrieved February 5, 2021.

386 Walsh, Matt. WALSH: I Looked Up Every Case Of An Unarmed Black Man Shot By Cops In 2019. Here's The Truth The Left Is Hiding. Dailywire, July 24, 2020.

387 Bolhken, Donald. What do the statistics, not the stereotypes, about killings by the police tell us? Des Moines Register, June 29, 2020.

388Marsh, Kristine. CNN's Rye Justifies Taking Police Weapons: 'Every Time We Don't Fight Back, We Die.' Newsbuster.org, June 15, 2021.

389 McCluney, Courtney, Robotham, Kathrina, Lee, Serenity, Smith, Richard, Durkee, Myles. The Costs of Code-Switching
The behavior is necessary for advancement — but it takes a great psychological toll. Harvard Business Review, November 15, 2019.

390 Harris, Ida. Code-Switching is Not trying to Fit in to White Culture, I'm Surviving it. Yes! December 17, 2019.

391 Number of people shot to death by the police in the United States from 2017 to 2020, by race Statista, January 5, 2020.

392 Owens, Candace. I Do Not Support George Floyd. Durtty Daily, June 4, 2020.

393 Judge dismisses 1 charge against former cop in George Floyd's death. Associated Press, TribLive, October 22, 2020

394 Gregorian, Dareh. Biden Says He Spoke to Jacob Blake. NBC, September 3, 2020.

395 Gravely, Michael. Report on the Officer involved shooting of Jacob Blake. County of Kenosha, 2021.

396 Pollack, Joel. Jacob Blake Sr. Has Long History of Racist, Antisemitic, Anti-Christian Posts; Set to Meet Joe Biden. Breitbart, September 2, 2020.

397 Flores, Terry. Damage due to rioting, unrest in Kenosha tops $50 million; 2,000 Guard assisted here. Kenoshanews, September 9, 2020.

398 Orrechio-Egresitz, Haven, Chaos will continue in Kenosha until the cop shot shot Jacob Black is fired or arrested local Black Lives Matter activists worry. Insider.com, August 24, 2020.

399 Kappeler, Victor, Gaines, Larry, Schaefer, Brian. Community Policing: A Contemporary Perspective. Routledge, 2020.

400 #Talkabouttrayvonmartin. Black Lives Matter, retrieved February 3, 2021.

401 Jabali, Malaika. If you're surprised by how the police are acting, you don't understand US history. The Guardian, June 5, 2020.

402 Fingerhut, Hannah. Deep racial, partisan divisions in Americans' views of police officers. Pew Research, September 15, 2017.

403 Officer Down Memorial Page. Odmp.org, retrieved February 5, 2021.

404 Voegeli, William. The Truth about White Flight. The City-Journal, Autumn 2020.

405 Williams, Walter. Opinion: The true plight of blacks in America. The Item, June 10, 2020.

406 Babwin, Don. Chicago ends 2020 with 769 homicides as gun violence surges. ABCnews, January 1, 2021.

407 Violent crimes surge in US as COVID-19 pandemic rages. Al Jazeera, December 28, 2020.

408 Jonsson, Patrick. 2020's murder increase is 'unprecedented.' But is it a blip? CS Monitor, December 14, 2020.

409 Known offender crosstabs. Ojjdp.gov, retrieved, January 29, 2021.

410 McDonald, Heather. Heather Mac Donald and Glenn Loury On Policing, Race, And Ideological Conformity. Manhattan Institute, October 6, 2020.

411 Malone, Justin. Uncle Tom. Movie, 2020.

412 Study finds largely Black cities are over- or under-policed. University or Oregon, December 14, 2020.

413 Howerton, Matt. D-FW gun stores still grappling with ammunition shortage after 2020 gun sales soar. ABC, WFAA.com, January 28, 2021.

414 Grzeszczak, Jocelyn.81% of Black Americans Don't Want Less Police Presence Despite Protests—Some Want More Cops: Poll. Newsweek, August 6, 2020.

415 McDonald, Heather. War on the Cops. Encounter Books, 2016.

416 McDonald, Heather. Manhattan Institute Heather McDonald on the use of police force. Chicago's Morning Answer, June 3, 2020.

417 Patterns and trends in household size and composition: Evidence from a United Nations dataset. United Nations: Department of Economic and Social Affairs Population Division, 2019.

418 Sanctuary Cities: A Threat to Public Safety. Hearing before the sub-Committee on Immigration and Border Security. July 23, 2015.

419 McIntyre, Douglas. Guns in America: Nearly 40 million guns were purchased legally in 2020 and another 4.1 million bought in January. USA Today, February 10, 2020.

420 Black doctor dies of Coivd-19 after claiming racist treatment. The Seattle Times, December 25, 2020.

421 Hamel, Liz, Lopez, Lunna, Manana, Cailey, Artiga, Samantha, Brodie, Mollyann. KFF/The Undefeated Survey on Race and Health. Kff.org, October 13, 2020.

Pettigrew, Thomas. Intergroup Prejudices: its causes and cures. Actualidades en Psicología 22(109):115, February 2011.

423 Lawrence E. M. Why Do College Graduates Behave More Healthfully than Those Who Are Less Educated? Journal of health and social behavior, 58(3), 291–306, 2017.

424 Hobson, Katherine. Racial And Ethnic Disparities Persist In Sudden Infant Deaths. NPR.com, May 15, 2017.

425 Infant Mortality among Black Babies. School of Public Health, University of Michigan, October 29, 2020.

426 Chen, A., Feresu, S. A., Fernandez, C., & Rogan, W. J. Maternal obesity and the risk of infant death in the United States. *Epidemiology (Cambridge, Mass.)*, 20(1), 74–81, 2009.

427 Rosenfeld, Samara. Higher Prepregnancy BMI Increases Rate of Infant Mortality. HCP Live, August 26, 2020.

428 Obesity and African Americans. Hhs.gov, retrieved January 1, 2021.

429 Minorityhealth.hhs.gov, retrieved February 9, 2021.

430 Births by Age and Race of Mother. Cdc.gov, retrieved January 1, 2021.

431 QuickStats: Infant Mortality Rates* for Single Births, by Age Group of Mother --- United States, 2006. CDC, Nov.26, 2010.

432 Quiñones, A. R., Botoseneanu, A., Markwardt, S., Nagel, C. L., Newsom, J. T., Dorr, D. A., & Allore, H. G. (2019). Racial/ethnic differences in multimorbidity development and chronic disease accumulation for middle-aged adults. PloS one, 14(6), e0218462.

433 Lack of exercise, not diet, linked to rise in obesity, Stanford research shows. Stanford Medicine, July 4, 2014.

434 Nutrition, Physical Activity, and Obesity. Healthypeople.gov, retrieved February 10, 2021.

Centers for Disease Control and Prevention. Prevalence of self-reported physically active adults - United States, 2007. MMWR Morb Mortal Wkly Rep. 2008;57(48):1297-1300.

435 Johnsgard, Keith. Conquering Depression & Anxiety through Exercise. Prometheus Books, 2004.

436 Liponis, Mark. Ultra-Longevity. Little Brown & Company, 2007.

437 Saffer, H., Dave, D., Grossman, M., & Leung, L. A. Racial, Ethnic, and Gender Differences in Physical Activity. Journal of human capital, 7(4), 378–410, 2013.

438 Otique, Darcie. Obesity among Black women outrageously high. The Atlanta Voice, November 15, 2019.

439 Rhoades, Jeffrey, Exercise in Adults, Age 18 and Older, in the United States, 2002: Estimates for the Noninstitutionalized Population. Medical Expenditure Panel Survey, February 2005.

440 Adults Who Report Participation in Any Physical Activity or Exercise by Race/Ethnicity. KFF.org, 2019.

441 Craig M. Hales, M.D., Margaret D. Carroll, M.S.P.H., Cheryl D. Fryar, M.S.P.H., and Cynthia L. Ogden, Ph.D. Prevalence of Obesity and Severe Obesity Among Adults: United States, 2017–2018, CDC, February 2020.

442 Zhang, Ni., Leary, Emily, Teti, Michelle, Stemmle, Jon, Hampton, Natalie. Examining the Factors That Influence African Americans in the Midwest to Reduce Salt Intake. HealthEquity Vol 4, No 1, May 12, 2020.

443 Adult Obesity Facts. CDC, retrieved January 1, 2021.

444 Overweight and Obesity Statistics. National Institute of Health, retrieved September 21, 2020.

445 Diabetes. Mayoclinic.com, retrieved January 1, 2021.

446 Minorityhealth.hhs.gov, retrieved February 9, 2021.

447 Muhammad, Khalil Gibran. 1619. NY Times Magazine, August 19, 2019.

[448] Zhang, Ni., Leary, Emily, Teti, Michelle, Stemmle, Jon, Hampton, Natalie. Examining the Factors That Influence African Americans in the Midwest to Reduce Salt Intake. HealthEquity Vol 4, No 1, May 12, 2020.

[449] High Blood Pressure and African Americans. Heaert.org, retrieved February 9, 2021.

[450] Airhihenbuwa, C., Kumanyika, S. Augurs, T., et al. Cultural aspects of African American easting patterns. Ethn. Health, 1:245-260, 1996.

[451] Woodson, Joyce M. M.S., R.D.; Brown-Gordon, Karen M.Ed.; Padilla-Loupias, Jennifer M.S.; Constantino, Nora Ph.D., FACSM Increasing Physical Activity in African Americans: A Multifaceted Approach, ACSM's Health & Fitness Journal: - Volume 14 - Issue 1 - p 16-22, January-February 2010.

[452] Fryar CD, Ostchega Y, Hales CM, Zhang G, Kruszon-Moran D. Hypertension prevalence and control among adults: United States, 2015–2016. NCHS data brief, no 289. Hyattsville, MD: National Center for Health Statistics. 2017.

[453] Getting Blood Pressure Under Control. CDC, September 2012.

[454] Racial and ethnic disparities in heart disease. CDC, April 2019.

[455] Statistics about diabetes. Diabetes.org, retrieved December 30, 2020.

[456] Obesity and cancer. National Cancer Institute, retrieved, January 1, 2021.

[457] Otique, Darcie. Obesity among Black women outrageously high. The Atlanta Voice, November 15, 2019.

[458] Mossey. JM. Defining racial and ethnic minorities in pain management. Clin Orthop Relat Res.469(7):1859-1870, 2011.

[459] Davis, Matthew. Blacks, whites, equally as likely to be prescribed opioids for pain. Institute for Healthcare Policy & Innovation, University of Michigan, May 1, 2018.

[460] Which Pre-Existing Conditions Put COVID-19 Patients Most at Risk of Death. US Pharmacist, October 21, 2020.

[461] Elfein, John. Distribution of COVID-19 (coronavirus disease) deaths in the United States as of January 27, 2021, by race. Statista, January 27, 2021.

[462] U.S. Renal Data System, USRDS 2016 Annual Data Report: Atlas of Chronic Kidney Disease and End-Stage Renal Disease in the United States, National Institutes of Health, National Institute of Diabetes and Digestive and Kidney Diseases, Bethesda, MD, 2016.

[463] Matsha, Tandi, Erasmis, Rajiv. Chronic Kidney Disease in sub-Saharan Africa. The Lancet, December 1, 2019.

[464] Kearney, Audrey, Lopes, Lunna, Brodie, Mollyann. Vaccine Hesitancy Among Hispanic Adults. KFF.com, January 14, 2021.

[465] Clinical Trials Have Far Too Little Racial and Ethnic Diversity. Scientific American, September 1, 2018.

[466] Flu Disparities Among Racial and Ethnic Minority Groups. CDC.gov, retrieved January 2, 2021.

[467] Flu & People with Diabetes. CDC.gov, retrieved January 2, 2021.

[468] Vaccine Effectiveness: How Well Do the Flu Vaccines Work? CDC.gov, retrieved January 2, 2021

[469] Vaccination Coverage Among Adults in the United States, National Health Interview Survey, 2016. CDC.gov, retrieved January 2, 2021.

[470] How to pay. Vaccines.gov, retrieved January 2, 2021.

[471] McDaniels, Andrea. Study: African Americans don't trust flu vaccine; whites don't think flu is that bad. Baltimore Sun, March 25, 2017.

[472] Snyder, V. N. S. de, Garcia, D., Pineda, R., Calderon, J., Diaz, D., Morales, A., & Perez, B. (2020). Exploring Why Adult Mexican Males Do Not Get Vaccinated: Implications for COVID-19 Preventive Actions. Hispanic Journal of Behavioral Sciences, 42(4), 515–527.

[473] Caratala, Sofia, Maxwell, Connor. Health Disparities by Race and Ethnicity. American Progress, May 7, 2020.

[474] Artiga, Samantha, Orgera, Kendall, Damico, Anthony. Changes in Health Coverage by Race and Ethnicity since the ACA, 2010-2018. KFF.org. March 5, 2020.

[475] Baumgartner, Jesse, Collins, Sara, Radley, David, Hayes, Susan. How the Affordable Care Act Has Narrowed Racial and Ethnic Disparities in Access to Health Care. The Commonwealth Fund, January 16, 2020.

[476] Cross-call, Jesse. Medicaid Expansion Has Helped Narrow Racial Disparities in Health Coverage and Access to Care. Center on Budget and Policy Priorities, October 21, 2020.

[477] Changes in Health Coverage by Race and Ethnicity since the ACA, 2010-2018. Kff.org, 2013, March 5, 2020.

[478] Conway, Douglas. Adults Age 26 Had Highest Uninsured Rate Among All Ages, Followed By 27-Year-Olds. Census.gov, October 26, 2020.

[479] Average Individual Health Insurance Premiums Increased 99% Since 2013, the Year Before Obamacare, & Family Premiums Increased 140%, According to eHealth.com Shopping Data, January 23, 2017.

[480] Probasco, Jim. Why Do Healthcare Costs Keep Rising? Investopedia, retrieved February 16, 2021.

[481] Diversity in Medicine: Facts and Figures 2019. AAMC.org.

[482] Ma, Jennifer Ma, Pender, Matea, Welch, Meredith. Education Pays 2019. College Board.

[483] Zahneis, Meghan. Why Has Black-Student Enrollment Fallen? Chronicle.com, August 18, 2019.

[484] The Economics Daily. Bureau of Labor Statistics, May 22, 2020.

[485] Status and Trends in Education of Racial and Ethnic Groups 2018. National Center for Education and Statistics, 2018.

[486] Indicator 23: Postsecondary Graduation Rates. National Center for Education Statistics, February 2019.

[487] Applicants to U.S. Medical Schools by Selected Combinations of Race/Ethnicity and Sex, 2017-2018 through 2020-2021. AAMC.org, retrieved February 5, 2021.

[488] Medical School Acceptance Rates by Race (2020): Does Ethnicity Play a Role? Shemmassian Academic Consulting, 2020.

[489] Total U.S. Medical School Enrollment by Race/Ethnicity (Alone) and Sex, 2016-2017 through 2020-2021. AAMC.org, retrieved January 2, 2021

[490] Average GPA and MCAT Score for Every Medical School (Updated in 2020). Shemmassian Academic Consulting.

[491] Perez-Stable, Eliseo. Communicating the Value of Race and Ethnicity in Research. National Institute of Health, June 27, 2018.

[492] Long, Jeffrey, C. Kittles, Rick. Human Genetic Diversity and the Nonexistence of Biological Races. Human Biology. 81 (5) 777-798, August, 2003.

[493] Schweninger, L. Prosperous Blacks in the South, 1790-1880. The American Historical Review, 95(1), 31-56, 1990.

[494] White, Shane. The Story of Wall Street's First Black Millionaire. The Atlantic, October 21, 2015.

[495] Huddleston, Tom. Mary Ellen Pleasant, one of the first black self-made millionaires, used an ingenious trick to build her fortune. CNBC.com, February 15, 2020.

[496] Zweigenhaft, Richard, Domhoff, William, Diversity in the Power Elite: How It Happened, Why It Matters. Rowman and Littlefield, April 10, 2006.

[497] Henry, Jim. Thomas Sowell on the root causes of income inequality. World.wng.org, December 30, 2014.

[498] Millionaires by race. Statista, retrieved December 26, 2020.

[499] Dilan, Kerry. America's richest self-made women. Forbes, October 13, 2020.

[500] Sowell, Thomas. Discrimination and Disparities. Basic Books, 2019.

[501] Williams, Walter. South Africa's War Against Capitalism. Praeger, 1989.

[502] McLanahan, Sara, Perchesk, Christine. Family Structure and the Reproduction of Inequalities. Office of Population Research, Princeton University, 2008.

[503] Poverty rate of Black families with a single mother in the United States 1990 to 2019. Statista, US Census, Bureau of Labor Statistics, retrieved February 17, 2021.

[504] Rowe, Ian. The power of the two-parent home is not a myth. Thomas Fordham Institute, January 8, 2020.

[505] Steele, Shelby. Interview. 'White Guilt' and the End of the Civil Rights Era. Npr.com, March 5, 2006.

[506] Cannato, Vincent. What Sets Italian-American immigrants off from other Immigrants. Humanities, Volume 36, Number 1, January/February 2015.

[507] "Can anyone stop Narendra Modi?" The Economist, April 5, 2014.

[508] Majumdar, Samirah. 5 Facts about religion in India. Pew Research, 2018.

[509] Prison Slaves. Al Jazeera, March 25, 2012.

[510] China: Extreme brainwashing at Uighur prison camps exposed in new leak. Deutche World, November 24, 2019.

[511] De La Roca, Jorge, Gould Ellen, Ingrid, Steil, Justin. Does Segregation Matter for Latinos? Journal of Housing Economics, 2018.

[512] Special Report- The Midwest: Separate, downtrodden. The Economist, July 25-31, 2020.

[513] Poorest Cities in the United States, 2011. Neoch.com, retrieved July 31, 2019.

[514] McCann, Adam. States with Most Racial Progress. Wallethub.com, January 14, 2020.

[515] Shambaugh, Jay, Nunn, Ray, Anderson, Stacy. How racial and regional inequality affect economic opportunity. Brookings.edu, February 15, 2019.

[516] Fisher, Max. A fascinating map of the world's most and least racially tolerant countries. Washington Post, May 15, 2013.

[517] Obama, Michelle. Becoming. Crown, 2018.

[518] Cashin, Sheryll. The Failures of Integration: How Race and Class are Undermining the American Dream. New York: Public Affairs, 2004.

[519] Aliprantis. Dionissi. Racial Inequality, Neighborhood Effects, and Moving to Opportunity. Federal Reserve Bank of Cleveland, November 4, 2019.

[520] Clark, William. Reexamining the Moving to Opportunity Study and its Contribution to Changing the Distribution of Poverty and Ethnic Concentration. National Institute of Health, August 2008.

[521] Cook, Lindsay. U.S. Education: Still Separate and Unequal. US News, January 28, 2015.

[522] Drop out rates. Kidscount Data Center, retrieved August 6, 2020.

[523] Educational attainment by race and ethnicity. American Council on Education, retrieved August 5, 2020.

[524] Williams, Walter. Opinion: The true plight of blacks in America. The Item, June 10, 2020.

[525] Myers, Dowell, Pitkin, John. Assimilation Today. American Progress, September 2010.

[526] Quillan, Lincoln, et al. Do Some Countries Discriminate More than Others? June 2019.

[527] Clark, Kevin. The Ten Best States for Black Household Wealth. Black Enterprise, September 19, 2014.

[528] Anderson, Monica, Lopez, Gustavo. Key Facts about black immigrants in the U.S. Pew Research Center, January 24, 2018.

[529] Anderson, Monica. Chapter 1: Statistical Portrait of the U.S. Black Immigrant Population. Pew Research, April 9, 2015.

[530] Wodtke G. T. The Impact of Education on Inter-Group Attitudes: A Multiracial Analysis. Social psychology quarterly, 75(1), 2012.

[531] Devaux, Marion, et al. "Exploring the Relationship Between Education and Obesity", OECD Journal: Economic Studies, Vol. 2011/1.